Illustrator:
Howard Chaney

Editor:
Charles Payne

Editor in Chief:
Sharon Coan, M.S. Ed.

Art Director:
Elayne Roberts

Art Coordination Assistant:
Cheri Macoubrie Wilson

Cover Artists:
Denise Bauer
Chris Macabitas

Product Manager:
Phil Garcia

Imaging:
Ralph Olmedo, Jr.

Acknowledgements:
HyperStudio® is a registered trademark of Roger Wagner Publishing, Inc.
ClarisWorks software and screenshots are © 1991–95 Claris Corporation. All Rights Reserved. *ClarisWorks* is a registered trademark of Claris Corporation in the U.S. and other countries.
Screen shot(s) reprinted with permission from Microsoft Corporation.
The Apple Logo, and Macintosh are trademarks of Apple Computer, Inc., registered in the United States and other countries.
The Writing Center™ is a registered trademark of The Learning Company.

Publishers:
Rachelle Cracchiolo, M.S. Ed.
Mary Dupuy Smith, M.S. Ed.

INTEGRATING TECHNO INTO THE CURRICULUM

CHALLENGING

Author:

Barb Thorson

Teacher Created Materials, Inc.
6421 Industry Way
Westminster, CA 92683
ISBN-1-55734-188-2
©1998 Teacher Created Materials, Inc.
Made in U.S.A.
Revised, 1999
www.teachercreated.com
URL updates available at our Web site.

TABLE OF CONTENTS

TABLE OF CONTENTS *(cont.)*

INTRODUCTION

Technology is exploding in our society and in our schools. *Integrating Technology into the Curriculum* will provide guidance and valuable information to empower teachers who want to integrate technology into their curriculum.

Part one of *Integrating Technology into the Curriculum* will focus on ideas to help organize technology in your classroom. The middle school curriculum is often departmentalized, and your school may or may not have a computer lab for the use of regular classroom teachers. In many middle schools, computer skills are taught by vocational teachers as a wheel subject, allowing students to have access to a computer for only short periods of time during the school year.

There are suggestions for the scheduling, planning, and management of one-computer and multi-computer classrooms. For those schools with computer labs or those planning a computer lab, diagrams have been included for organizing the labs.

With an emphasis on school improvement and accountability, teachers are looking for assessment tools. Ideas for assessing student projects, such as checklists and rubrics, have been provided within these pages, as well as suggestions for teacher, peer, and self-assessment.

Part two of *Integrating Technology into the Curriculum* offers concrete ideas for enhancing the curriculum through projects on the computer. Included are lessons which integrate technology into language arts, math, math and science, science, science and health, social studies, and special areas. Each lesson includes a topic, subject area, lesson plan, advanced organizers for the student, and assessment recommendations for the teacher. Each lesson plan also recommends software and includes helpful tips for teaching the lesson.

Cost is always a factor in purchasing software, and the lessons in this book are adaptable to software you may already have access to in your schools. *Integrating Technology into the Curriculum* is an excellent resource for classroom teachers looking for ways to use technology to extend the middle school curriculum.

HARDWARE

WHAT IS IT?

Simply put, hardware is any computer technology that one can touch. The computer, printer, monitors, keyboard, and mouse are all hardware components. These are mechanisms that carry the instructions that the software gives. This section will provide background on the capabilities of different pieces of hardware. Each piece of hardware and its function are described.

COMPUTERS

CHOOSING A COMPUTER

Much like choosing an automobile, choosing a computer can be a daunting task. There are several manufacturers that package computers in hundreds of ways. They use model numbers and slick names to steer us away from "what's under the hood."

PLATFORM

Platform refers to the type of computer/operating system being used. There are two major choices: Windows or Macintosh (DOS ships standard on all IBM and compatibles). In the past this was a major decision when considering a purchase, in that IBM and compatible machines could not run Macintosh programs and vice versa. With the development of software translators and dual platform machines (they can run software for both platforms), the problem has become less significant. However, this is still a consideration. Here are a few questions that will help a teacher or school make the platform decision.

1. What platform is shared by the people with whom documents are most often shared (office staff, fellow teachers, school sites)? If only one is used, choose that platform. If both are utilized, choose a platform that can easily operate in both environments.

2. What platform offers the software currently in use or under consideration? Most companies produce software versions for both platforms; however, because of the abundance of IBM compatibles, Windows and DOS software is more readily accessible through retailers. Macintosh software, although available, tends to be easier to get through mail order sources such as Mac Mall, Mac Warehouse, and educational suppliers.

PROCESSOR

The brain of any computer is its processor. The ability to handle large computing jobs with speed and accuracy depends largely on the processor. Computer manufacturers have evolved through several microprocessors, each generation faster and more powerful than the last. Don't focus on the name or model number of the microprocessor. Compare the speed of the processor with other models in an acceptable price range. The computing speed of a processor is listed in megahertz or MHz.

Another thing to consider is upgradability. Many manufacturers now offer microprocessor upgrades that are as simple as removing the old processor from the motherboard and plugging a new one in place. This is an inexpensive way to keep computer equipment from becoming obsolete and leaves the computer system and peripherals intact.

COMPUTERS *(cont.)*

STORAGE

Storage is the amount of long-term memory that a computer can file or store. There are many kinds of storage devices on the market, including hard disk drives, magneto-optical drives, tape drives, and CD–ROM. Storage is measured in megabytes (MB) or gigabytes (GB). There are 1,000 megabytes in a gigabyte. Almost all computers now come with an internal hard disk drive and at least one removable disk drive, such as a floppy drive.

RAM

RAM or random access memory is the computer's short-term memory, which it needs to carry out a program's instructions. As software becomes more and more memory intensive, it is important to buy a computer with enough RAM to handle it. RAM's unit of measure is the megabyte or MB. Here are a few questions to ask when considering a purchase:

1. How much RAM does the operating system software use? Windows and MacOS require a large amount of RAM just to run the computer.

2. What types of programs will be run? Graphic-intensive programs like educational CD-ROMs require several megabytes of RAM to run. Check the minimum RAM requirements for the software that is being used or considered, and then add at least 25% more as a safety net.

3. Will more than one program be running at a time? Many first-time computer users don't see the need to have multiple programs running; however, the time savings of being able to move information from one program to another is extremely useful. Add the minimum memory requirements for the programs likely to be open simultaneously and add 25% for safety.

4. Is the RAM easily upgradable, and what is the maximum RAM upgradability? As computer programs are developed that require more memory, it is important to be able to "keep up."

PERIPHERALS

Peripherals are things that are added to the computer, such as printers, scanners, modems, video input cards, digital cameras, etc., that enhance what it can do. When shopping for peripherals, study the job that the peripheral will accomplish and the software needed to do it. Ask the following questions:

1. What quality is realistically expected?

2. Will anything need to be added to the computer in order for the peripheral to work?

3. Does the peripheral require any software not included with it?

MAINTENANCE

Computers require very little maintenance other than the occasional cleaning of the circuit boards inside the case, as well as the exterior. The cleaning of the interior of the computer is best left to a properly trained professional. Most importantly, never come in direct contact with the interior of the computer without taking antistatic measures. Static electricity discharged in a computer can cause severe damage.

INPUT DEVICES

Input devices are items that allow the user to interact or input information into the computer. Input devices include the keyboard, mouse, touch pad, trackball, graphics tablet, scanner, digital camera, touchscreen, and microphone.

KEYBOARD

There are several keyboards on the market in a wide range of prices. Most fall into two categories: standard and extended. Standard keyboards are similar to most typewriter keyboards except for a few additional keys that are necessary to carry out extra functions that are assigned by the software. Extended keyboards add several other function keys, as well as a numeric calculator type keypad. These are preferable, especially if math concepts are taught with the computer.

PORTABLE KEYBOARDS

Several manufacturers have developed portable keyboards that allow the student to enter and edit text and then transfer it to a computer for formatting and printing. These relatively inexpensive machines are perfect for classrooms which do not have enough computers to allow the students enough keyboard time. For example, the student can write a story or report on the keyboard, do the preliminary editing, and then "dump" the text into the computer's word processor. From there the student can spell check, format, add pictures, and print the document. Since the initial keyboarding is the most time consuming of these tasks, the portable keyboard saves precious computer time at a fraction of the cost of a computer. Other models even allow the user to connect directly to a printer, allowing a student to print out the text for editing prior to publishing with a computer.

MOUSE

Named because of its resemblance to the rodent, the mouse is an input device that controls the cursor on the screen. The ball on the underside rolls against smooth gears which, in turn, send a signal to the computer and control the cursor. Mice come in several configurations containing from one to three buttons. Once the user has the cursor where he or she wants it, the button or buttons on the top of the mouse can be clicked to move the cursor or select an item or items. The mouse works best on a mouse pad. Better mouse pads are made of dense foam rubber with a non-slide surface on the table side and a tightly woven cloth material on the side that comes in contact with the mouse.

TOUCH PAD

A touch pad is a device that is an alternative to a mouse. Instead of rolling a mouse around, the user moves the tip of his or her finger on the surface of the pad. The cursor reacts much as it does with a mouse.

INPUT DEVICES *(cont.)*

GRAPHICS TABLET

A graphics tablet is a device on which the user can draw freehand while the drawing is duplicated on the computer screen. Aside from the use in a graphics environment, this type of device comes in handy when teachers are presenting using the computer. For instance, if a picture is shown on the computer or large screen projection device, the teacher can use the tablet to circle or make notes right on the screen. Sports commentators use these same devices to call attention to details on a replay by drawing directly on the screen.

TOUCHSCREEN

Very useful for special needs children who have underdeveloped fine motor coordination, the touch-screen is an overlay to the monitor. When accompanied with the appropriate software, users touch the screen to make the selection they require in a program. These are widely used in informational kiosks (e.g., wedding registers at major department stores).

MICROPHONES

With the proliferation of multimedia computers and the use of recorded sound has evolved the ability to record oneself on the computer. In addition, many new computers have a voice recognition capability. Many computers have microphones built in to do this, although the quality and flexibility of these is not usually very good. Several electronics stores sell microphones starting at as little as five dollars. Any of these will work as long as the plug is the right size. Most computers accept the mini-plug, one-eighth inch diameter.

SCANNERS

Scanners are peripheral devices that can take an image from the printed medium and digitize it for use in a computer. For instance, if a class is writing reports about ancient Greece and the textbook has an excellent picture of the Parthenon, a scanner can be used to save the image for use in reports. If the scanner has OCR (optical character recognition) software, scanned text can be used in a word processor and may be edited just as if it had been typed in.

DIGITAL CAMERAS

There are several digital cameras on the market that allow students and teachers to take pictures and bring them directly from the devices into the computer. Since the cameras save the image in a digital format, they require no film. The pictures are stored as numbers in the memory of the camera. The memory can be transferred from the camera to the computer through a cable. The computer software can then assemble the digital information into an image that can be used in a variety of writing and presentation programs. These cameras are available in models which produce either black and white or color images. Some models are portable, with the ability to be taken anywhere; whereas, others require the connection of a computer in order to be utilized.

OUTPUT DEVICES

Output devices are mechanisms that allow the user to receive some type of product from a computer. Examples of output devices are printers, monitors, large screen projectors, and speakers.

MONITORS

A monitor is the screen for the computer. They are available in many sizes and configurations. To take advantage of programs rich in multimedia (text, sound, animation, video, photographs, drawings, etc.), a good quality monitor that supports at least 256 colors is a necessity. Monitors that support thousands and millions of colors are also available. Be aware that high-end, large-screen monitors will require the addition of special parts called "video cards" installed into a computer.

Size

Monitors, like TVs, come in several different sizes. The measurement of a monitor is a straight diagonal line from corner to corner of the screen. Most home and school computers are a 13"–15" (32.5 cm–38 cm) diagonal picture. Prices of monitors over 15" (38 cm) increase rapidly and are usually overkill for student use unless used for school newspaper or yearbook layout.

Resolution

The resolution of the picture refers to the amount of tiny pixels (or lights) there are on a monitor screen. This is usually expressed in a number sentence that shows the dimensions of the screen in pixels (e.g., 640 x 480). The greater the number of pixels, the truer the picture is on the screen.

High Resolution Video Cards

High resolution video cards are required to display high resolution computer images on larger monitors. The circuit board that is installed inside a computer contains VRAM or video random access memory. This memory is there solely for the purpose of allowing images to be drawn on the screen without slowing down other computer operations.

PROJECTION DEVICES

High-End Multimedia Projectors

These large-screen projectors are incredible and incredibly priced, usually between $3,000 to $10,000. These pieces of equipment are used to project computer, video, and laserdisc images onto a large movie screen. They are portable and usually include a built-in sound system.

LCD Panels

Liquid crystal display, or LCD panels, work using the same technology as the digital watches many of us own. In an LCD, the liquid crystals float between two sheets of glass that are embedded with electrodes. This panel is then placed on an overhead projector, connected to a computer or video source, and projected onto a large screen. These devices are still very expensive for use in a single classroom, with the average price ranging from just under $1,000 for a black-and-white model to several thousand for the top-of-the-line active matrix color model. In addition, most of these panels will require a special, extra-bright overhead projector, which is an additional cost.

OUTPUT DEVICES *(cont.)*

Projecting on a TV

Displaying an image on a TV is a very good way to use the computer as a presentation tool. Whether teaching the class how to use a program or as a visual aid for a science lesson, it is advantageous to connect a computer to a television.

Projecting with older computers

A more affordable option for large-screen projection is the television. The Apple II, Laser, Radio Shack, and Commodore computers popular in the 1980s used regular video line signals. Because of this, these computers are very easy to display on a large-screen television. Split the video line coming out of the back of the computer by attaching a "Y" cable. This allows the computer to be seen at both its monitor and on the television. Anything that is seen on the television can also be videotaped.

Projecting with newer computers

In order to accomplish the higher resolution graphics we are used to on today's computers, computer companies such as IBM and Apple moved away from line video used for television signals. Because of this, special hardware called "video conversion" or print-to-video boxes are needed to convert these high resolution video signals to those which can be handled by televisions. These boxes are much more affordable than other large-screen projection devices. If televisions and VCRs are available, they give the user the added dimension of being able to videotape student presentations and projects for replay at school or home.

AV Input/Output Cards

Some computers are equipped or can be installed with AV cards. These circuit boards allow the connection of audio and video equipment such as VCRs, video cameras, laserdisc players, audio CD players, and tape recorders. When connected to appropriate equipment and running appropriate software, these AV cards can record audio and video clips for use in multimedia presentations by students or teachers. If the card has an output capability, the computer can be linked directly to a TV, VCR, or tape recorder. Computer sounds and images can then be viewed or recorded. This eliminates the need for a separate print-to-video box.

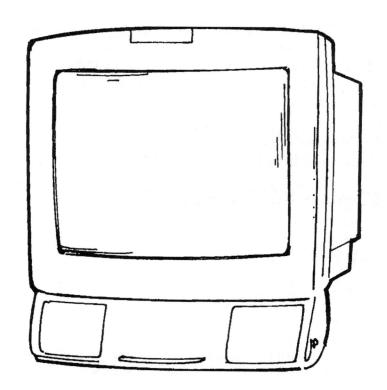

OUTPUT DEVICES *(cont.)*

PRINTERS

There are several brands of printers on the market. However, there are only three types of printers most commonly found in schools: dot matrix, ink jet, and laser.

Dot Matrix Printers

Dot matrix printers are characterized by very fast printing at a lower visual quality than other printers. A dense grid of metal pins impact against an ink ribbon to form the shapes of letters and symbols. It takes several pins to make the shape of a letter. Most of these printers are equipped with tractor and friction feed. Tractor feed requires a continuous roll of special paper with holes on either side that engage in the gears of the printer for advancement. "Friction feed" means that the paper can be fed through the printer by friction, much like a typewriter.

Ink-Jet Printers

Ink jet printers are very popular because of their flexibility. Although slower than dot matrix, ink-jet printers can print type and pictures in shades of gray and with some models, even in color. These printers work by spraying ink through very small jets in order to form the shape and shade required. Color ink jets combine layers of red, green, and blue to achieve different hues and shades.

Laser Printers

Laser printers work much like photocopiers. A thin layer of toner powder is distributed over the surface of the paper. A laser draws the shapes and increases or decreases the intensity of the light in order to achieve shading. The toner which is hit by the laser adheres to the paper, and the rest is removed.

SPEAKERS

Most computers purchased in the last five years are equipped with or have the capability of producing sound. In order to produce sound, computers must have a sound card installed. The presence of a sound card can usually be identified by looking for a speaker jack at the back panel of the computer. This is usually labeled with the word "speaker" or an icon that represents it. Computer speakers must be amplified in order to be heard. Make sure that amplified speakers are specified when purchasing.

COMMUNICATION DEVICES

In order to communicate with other computers, a computer requires either a modem or network card. The use of a modem or network card depends on the computer's connectivity (the way in which computers are connected).

NETWORK CARDS

If a school's computer is networked, the computer will require a network card similar to those used throughout the school. These devices allow a computer to share files, share devices (like printers), and communicate with one another. If a network is directly connected to the Internet, the network card will allow access to information on other computers and networks around the world.

OUTPUT DEVICES *(cont.)*

MODEMS

Most schools, however, do not have the resources for such costly connections to the Internet. In this case, modems are used to make this connection. These devices can be internal, inside the computer in the form of a circuit board, or external, in the form of a box that is connected to the rear of the computer by a cable. The devices translate the digital information that a computer understands to analog or sound information that can be sent over a normal phone line. Because this translation takes time, modems are typically slower than directly connecting to a network. Modems are, however, much less expensive than the infrastructure required for a network. In order to access the Internet, one would only need a modem, a dedicated phone line, and an Internet service provider (ISP). When shopping for a modem, one should look at the rate at which it can send and receive information. This is known as the baud rate and is expressed in bytes per second (bps). The industry standard is 33,000 bps, or 33.6K bps as of the date that this book was published.

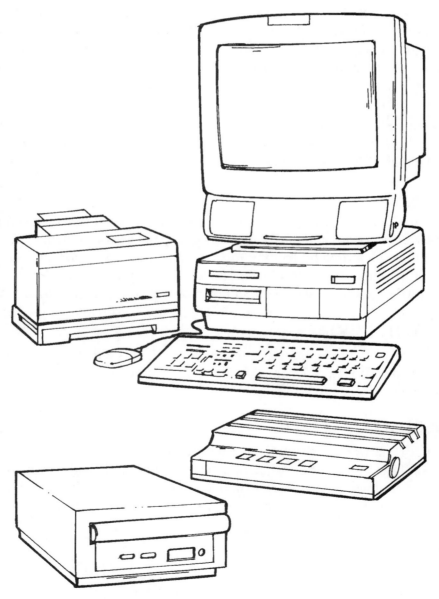

THE COMPUTER LAB

A common way to arrange computers in a middle school is to organize them into a computer lab. Traditionally, the computer lab is a room that has been designed for the housing and operation of a school's computers. It may be managed by a computer professional who may or may not be a teacher. In the past, computer labs were places to perform "drill and skill" activities, but these labs are slowly metamorphosing into technology centers—places where multimedia projects are created, telecommunications are taking place, presentations are made, and student television broadcasts are captured on film. Computer labs are assuming a role similar to the media center, becoming a hub of school activity. It is, therefore, necessary to take some things into account when equipping a technology lab.

PHILOSOPHY

What is the school's philosophy of technology in education? Some educators feel that technology plays a very minor role, while others feel it is crucial to prepare students to operate in today's workplace. The school as a community must decide the role technology should play in the lives of students. The technology lab, in both its equipment and its mission, should reflect these principles.

PURPOSE

What is the purpose of technology in the education of students? Quite often teachers see computers as something extra to do once the business of learning has taken place. It is important to realize that a computer is a tool to help students and teachers accomplish something better, neater, faster, and more efficiently; it is not a toy to play with when meaningful work is done.

SOFTWARE

There is currently a debate about the presence of instructional versus productivity software. Instructional software takes a concept and extends or reinforces it. Some instructional software programs have amazing simulations and problem-solving activities, while others are no better than expensive workbooks put on the computer. Productivity software is primarily designed and used as a tool. It helps teachers and students create a product, such as a word processed document, a piece of art, or a multimedia presentation. So. . . what should be emphasized in the classroom? The answer to that question will be based on a school's philosophy, but both kinds of software have a unique place in classroom integration.

EQUIPMENT

Many schools are readying themselves to jump on the integrated technology bandwagon. What is to be done if most of its equipment is outdated and cannot run much, if any, of the desired software? It is never too early to begin planning and to make the shift to newer technology. Begin teacher training and get the support of parent groups. It is amazing how much can be raised with bake sales and craft fairs if only the parent population is involved. Also, look into educational technology magazines for available grants. Technology is receiving a great deal of interest and funding right now—possibilities just need to be discovered and pursued.

SCHEDULING

There are many options available when scheduling teacher slots in a computer lab. The most common seems to be a fixed schedule, but flexible scheduling is becoming more popular as the use of technology increases in middle schools. Each school has different needs. Investigate the different scheduling options available and choose the one that fits the school's needs best.

THE FIXED SCHEDULE

This is currently the most common scheduling method in schools, where every open slot in the lab is filled with a class. This schedule repeats itself week after week. Each class in the school attends the lab a regular number of times each week.

Advantages of a Fixed Schedule:

- A fixed schedule sets a routine for the teacher and students by creating a set lab time every week.
- Fixed schedules ensure equitable distribution of lab time.
- Teachers cannot lose time slots because they forgot to sign up or there were no convenient times.

Disadvantages of a Fixed Schedule:

- Teachers are not able to sign up for more lab time for large projects if needed.
- Students may see working on the computer as just a part of their routine instead of thinking of it as a tool for its true purpose—to create a better product than they can create without it.

Weekly Schedule

TIME	MON	TUES	WED	THUR	FRI
9:00-9:50	JOHNSON	BARKER	MORSE	SMART	COHEN
9:50-10:40	CARTER	SMART	HARRIS	MEDFORD	TERRY
10:40-11:30	MEDFORD	TERRY	CHANG	HARRIS	DOBER
12:00-12:50	DOBER	COHEN	JOHNSON	CARTER	GREEN
12:50-1:30	BARKER	MORSE	GREEN	CHANG	

SCHEDULING *(cont.)*

THE FLEXIBLE SCHEDULE

Flexible scheduling is different from a fixed schedule because it changes from week to week. All of the open slots in a lab are shared among all teachers. A flexible schedule allows teachers to sign up for slots as needed instead of being tied into a certain time slot every week. For example, if a teacher is creating a *HyperStudio* presentation as the culminating activity in a social studies unit, it may take six or more visits to the computer lab. This could spread the project out over many weeks—long past the end of the unit. With flexible scheduling, a teacher can schedule those six slots in the lab as needed over a one- or two-week period while the students are involved in the topic in the classroom.

Time	Monday	Tuesday	Wednesday	Thursday	Friday
9:00–9:50	Jones	Jones	Jones	Julius	Jones
9:50–10:40	Feldman	Julius	Jones	Preez	Preez
10:40–11:30	Feldman	Pittman	Pittman	Pittman	Preez
11:30–12:00	Santelli	Terry	Preez	Terry	Terry
12:00–12:50	Alexander	Terry	O'Boyle	Oxford	O'Boyle
12:50–1:40	Minter	Minter	Minter	Minter	O'Boyle
1:40–2:30	Cornell	Oxford	Oxford	Alexander	Cornell
2:30–3:10	Bryant	Bryant	Bryant	Bryant	Byrant

ADVANTAGES OF A FLEXIBLE SCHEDULE:
- Teachers have more flexibility in scheduling.
- A flexible schedule allows in-depth projects to be completed in a timely manner.
- This ensures optimum use of the lab—teachers sign up for specific projects instead of looking for something to do in the lab at the last minute.
- Teachers who depend on a routine may sign up for the same time each week.

DISADVANTAGES OF A FLEXIBLE SCHEDULE:
- Students may not have time in the computer lab every single week.
- Teachers who are less comfortable in the lab may not sign up as often.
- Teachers may not get time slots that fit best into their schedules.

SCHEDULING *(cont.)*

Fixed schedules have been easily used and understood in middle schools for years. Generally, a committee of teachers and administrators work together to place teachers into fixed weekly slots that do not conflict with their lunchtimes or special classes. There are several organizational points to keep in mind if a school is interested in switching to a flexible scheduling method. Below is a guide to help implement flexible scheduling.

Count the number of slots available per week in the computer lab. These can be divided by teacher, or by grade level, giving some grade levels more slots in the lab.

For example, for a school with 40 slots per week in the computer lab, the lab may have sign-ups by six-week, nine-week, or 12-week periods, depending on how the school is organized and how far ahead teachers want to plan. (It is recommended to NOT schedule week by week in order to avoid the risk of teachers putting their projects off until the end of the scheduling period and making a mad rush for lab time.) This example examines a school that has lab sign-up every six weeks.

Time	Monday	Tuesday	Wednesday	Thursday	Friday
9:00–9:50					
9:50–10:40					
10:40–11:30					
11:30–12:00					
12:00–12:50					
12:50–1:40					
1:40–2:30					
2:30–3:10					

If your school used this exact schedule, you would have 240 slots to offer during those six weeks (40 slots per week multiplied by six weeks).

TIME SLOT DISTRIBUTION

- The distribution could be broken down by the number of teachers: If there are 24 teachers, each teacher will get ten time slots.
- It could be broken down by grade level, evenly or unevenly (e.g., eighth grade teachers use more advanced technology with students and need more time for complex projects).

EVENLY
Grade 6: 80 time slots
Grade 7: 80 time slots
Grade 8: 80 time slots

UNEVENLY
Grade 6: 70 time slots
Grade 7: 70 time slots
Grade 8: 100 time slots

SCHEDULING *(cont.)*

LAB SIGN-UP

Sign-up day in the lab could take place at the beginning of each six weeks. The lab schedule for each week is placed on a clipboard or spread out on a table. Teachers plan computer projects that integrate technology into their classroom curriculum prior to this sign-up day. When they come, they are able to sign up on consecutive days for large projects and then space the rest of their time slots over the six weeks to complete smaller word processing projects or quick lessons.

Some schools organize their system by vouchers. Each open time slot is a voucher. The vouchers (slips of paper that guarantee entrance into the computer lab) are divided among the teachers, and they must take in a voucher each time they visit the computer lab.

In some schools, teachers barter for and trade their vouchers from scheduling period to scheduling period. For example, Mrs. Pittman knows she is doing an intense project this period and may need up to 14 slots; she can trade her vouchers (time slots) with Mrs. Julius so that this six weeks, Mrs. Pittman has 14 slots and Mrs. Julius has six. For the next scheduling rotation, Mrs. Pittman will have six time slots, and Mrs. Julius will have 14. This allows teachers more flexibility to produce more complex (and even better quality) projects in the lab.

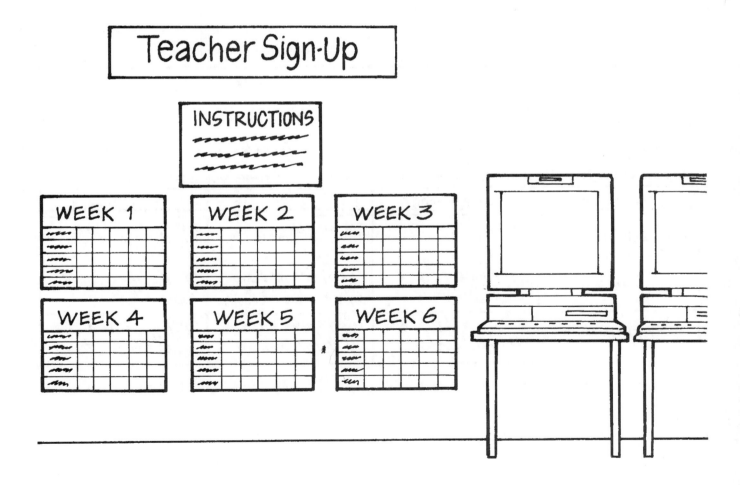

SCHEDULING *(cont.)*

LAB ATTENDANCE

Record which teachers or grade levels are using the lab with a Lab Attendance Record (page 19). There is a place for each teacher's name, date, and class project. This document will help show how often the lab is being used and what each class is doing in the lab. Because this document will be available to everyone using the lab, teachers will be able to see what is being produced by other classes. Teachers who primarily use the lab for word processing may see that other teachers are creating number concept slide shows and may have their classes try it. See the reproducible attendance record on the next page. A sample attendance record might look like this:

LAB ATTENDANCE RECORD

Please write the date and project in progress each time you use this lab.

Teacher Name	Date/Project	Date/Project	Date/Project

EXAMPLE:

Please write the date and project in progress each time you attend the lab

Teacher Name	Date/Project	Date/Project	Date/Project
Butler	9/4 Publishing Story	9/8 Publishing Story	9/8 Parts of Speech Activity
Jones	9/5 Ancient Egypt Slide Show	9/6 Ancient Egypt Slide Show	9/7 Ancient Egypt Slide Show
Pittman	9/3 Hyper Card the Skeletal System	9/4 Hyper Card the Skeletal System	9/5 Hyper Card the Skeletal System

As teachers sign in their individual classes, they can see what other teachers are doing in the lab and share ideas.

SCHEDULING *(cont.)*

LAB ATTENDANCE RECORD

Please write the date and project in progress each time you use this lab.

Teacher Name	Date/Project	Date/Project	Date/Project	Date/Project	Date/Project	Date/Project

PLANNING

There are many ready-made technology lessons within this book for those who are just getting started using technology. As teachers become more proficient with the use of technology, they may want to create their own technology lessons based on the students' needs as well as their own objectives.

Many teachers are overwhelmed at the thought of planning technology lessons for their classrooms, especially if they are inexperienced, unprepared, or untrained. After awhile, they will find that planning technology is as easy as helping students plan any other project from a book report to a science project. Begin with the curriculum. What is happening in the classroom? Start with the objectives for the unit or lesson and then think of ways a computer can help students express what they have learned. Many teachers begin with a software program and ask themselves, "What can my students do with this?" It is much easier to begin with the objectives and the content and ask the question, "What technology tools can I use to help my students reach these goals?" That way teachers can be sure that they are using technology to enhance the curriculum and not trying to modify lessons to fit the available technology.

Use the Technology Lesson Plan Advance Organizer (page 22) as a guide. However, feel free to change the planning sheet to meet specific needs. One excellent use of this planning sheet is as a tool for communication. If a school does not yet have a technology coordinator, this advance organizer for teachers can be a great way to share ideas among staff. Each time a teacher uses the planning sheet to create a lesson for his or her students, he or she can make a copy of the lesson plan to be housed in a notebook in the library or computer lab. Be sure to make copies of the assessment model used or any advance organizers needed by the students. If all teachers create lesson plans, this notebook can be a wonderful resource. If a teacher is ever stumped for an idea, he or she can see what other teachers have been doing. Organize the notebook by subject level so teachers can find things easily. It may be a little work in the beginning, but it will save work in the end by providing a fountain of ideas.

IDEAS FOR PLANNING

Plan lessons with specialists.

Combine the talents of classroom teachers, media specialists, technology specialists, and other specialists at school. Plan activities that span the curriculum and reach beyond the confines of the classroom. A great deal of research will be done outside of the classroom, so involve those teachers who will be helping along the way. The media specialist may have a unique way to complete the research for a particular topic and provide insight to the best way to organize it.

PLANNING *(cont.)*

IDEAS FOR PLANNING *(cont.)*

Make joint plans with the teachers on the same grade level.

For example, set aside one morning a month to brainstorm ideas for integrating technology into one grade level's curriculum. Have teachers share what they have done and what they would like to do with their students. It is amazing to find that many teachers share the same concerns, and it is much easier to find solutions together than everyone struggling alone.

Plan across the different grade levels.

If several people at the school are interested in technology, form a committee to create a database of good technology ideas for school. Many ideas in this book can be used on multiple grade levels. Sixth graders could benefit from technology ideas used on the seventh grade level. Occasionally, teachers avoid this approach because they are afraid of their students repeating the same projects year after year. In actuality, this process can enhance the learning experience by reinforcing previously learned skills with new guidelines and added requirements. For example, say a sixth grade teacher utilizes the lesson plan for determining the genre of a work of fiction. The sixth grade class project would include a general discussion of genres and writing a report on the genre of a specific book or books. The seventh grade teacher, however, could utilize the same lesson plan to introduce students to the historical evolution of genres. The development of the novel, the short story, and narrative poetry could all be researched, culminating in a writing activity where students try their hand at a chosen genre. The eighth grade class could take the process a step further, developing a Web page, publishing student examples of genres, and displaying links to other literature sites (teacher-approved, of course). It is possible that a technology lesson can be modified to be utilized for multiple grade levels.

Plan with teachers from other schools.

Use the resources available within the school district. Find other teachers who are excited about technology and share ideas. Students may even become Internet pen pals, corresponding by e-mail with students in other schools and school districts.

PLANNING *(cont.)*

TECHNOLOGY LESSON PLAN ADVANCE ORGANIZER

Teacher: _____

Topic: _____

Subject: _____

Program(s): _____

Assessment:

_____ Rubric for teacher evaluation

_____ Rubric for peer evaluation

_____ Checklist

_____ Anecdotal

_____ Other

Teacher Objectives and Focus Points:

(These are the skills that are being targeted with this project. Examples: research skills, organization skills, facts, artwork, graphics, writing, creativity, etc.)

  1.

  2.

  3.

Major Content Covered in the *Project* (not the entire unit):

(Examples: If it is a project on the Civil War, include any one or more of the following: battles, generals, uniforms, important women, important minorities, causes and effects, major turning points, etc. For a human body project, include the major bones with interesting facts about the skeletal system.)

  1.

  2.

  3.

Project Requirements:

(other things to be included, such as maps, sounds, or scanned pictures)

MANAGEMENT

As the computer lab becomes a more integral part of elementary education, it will become a hub of student and staff activity. Teachers needing instructional and technical assistance need to know they can find it in the computer lab. However, you do not have to be a computer expert to provide this help; you only need to have the desire. As a professional maintaining a computer lab, many things may fall under your jurisdiction—from software installation or minor technical problems to joint planning of technology lessons and, finally, staff development.

Here are some useful management ideas to help keep your computer lab running smoothly throughout the year. (If you do not have a computer lab at your elementary school, you may wish to use some of these ideas in your media center or teacher resource room.)

COMPUTER LAB SETUP

If you wish to make your computer lab truly a technology lab, do not think of it as just a place to use a computer. It should be a center of student productivity. Include stations for video capture and editing, telecommunicating, publishing, and more.

If possible, for behavior management purposes, arrange the computers around the perimeter of the room. This allows the person facilitating the activity to do a quick scan of who is on task.

Student Stations

- Provide your students with computer clipboards (the clips that hold your notes comfortably on the side of your computer). Student projects require notes, research, planning sheets—all kinds of information for students to reference while working. This helps students keep their personal areas organized while helping them get their work done. (For right-handed students these should be mounted on the left side of the computer monitor; for left-handed students they should be mounted on the right. Most manufacturers offer a Velcro attachment so the clipboard can be switched, if necessary.)

- Do not forget about left-handed students. Show them how to switch the mouse to the left side of the keyboard (if possible on your hardware). Another option is to set up a couple of permanent stations for left-handed students. Quite often, left-handed students will not complain about the difficulty of using a mouse with their right hands, but try to make it easy for them by making a few minor adjustments.

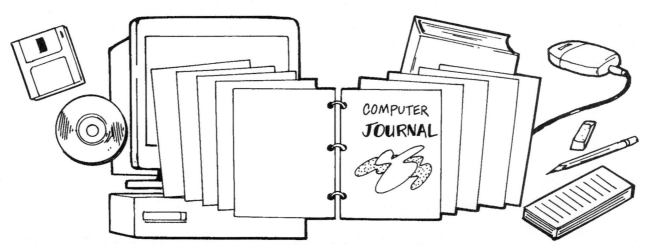

MANAGEMENT *(cont.)*

COMPUTER LAB SETUP

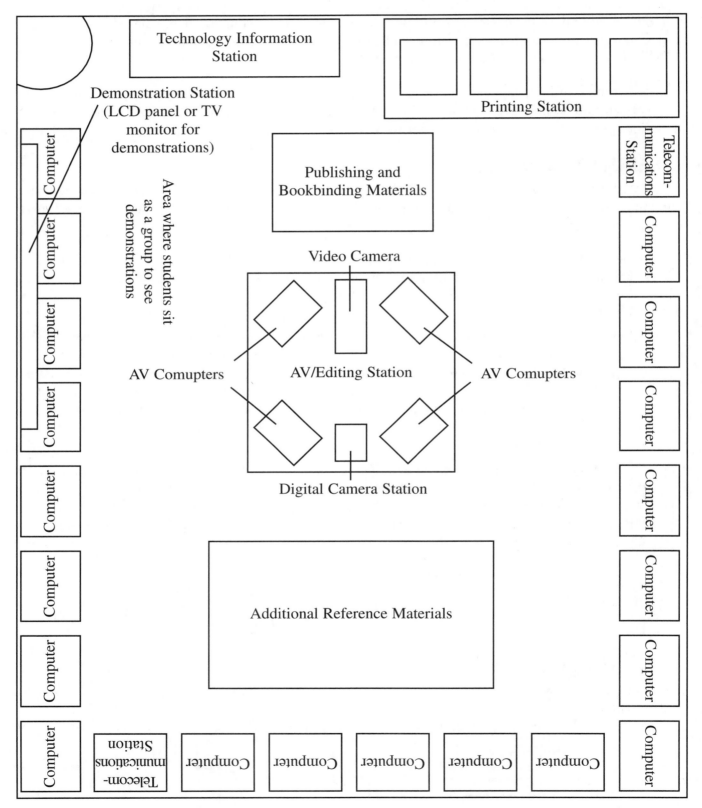

MANAGEMENT *(cont.)*

INFORMATION STATION

Throughout the day, teachers may need assistance ranging from questions about software to computer problems. Set up a help area near the entrance door to your lab to minimize lab interruption. Here they can sign up for lab times, get lesson plan ideas, request assistance, and answer their own software questions.

Contents of Information Station:

- Teacher Update Board
- Technology Lesson Plan Binder
- Software Manuals
- Software Help Binder
- Schedule Clipboard

- Lab Attendance Record
- Computer Maintenance Request Clipboard
- Software Inventory Clipboard
- Software Licensing Binder

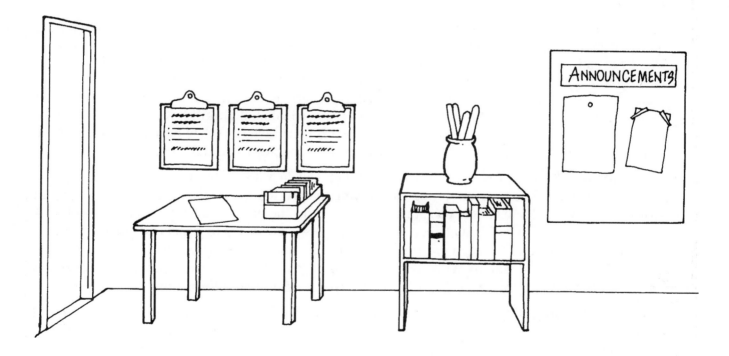

TEACHER UPDATE BOARD

If you do not have an electronic mail system for your staff, it can be very difficult to keep teachers up-to-date with new information and announcements related to technology. Hang a white board or a bulletin board at the information station to keep teachers informed about happenings in the computer lab. Here you can inform teachers of upcoming staff development opportunities in your school or outside of your school, technology conferences, deadlines for student projects, upcoming computer club or technology committee meetings, student software orders, and other important announcements.

MANAGEMENT *(cont.)*

CLIPBOARDS

- **Schedule Clipboard:** Keep your computer lab schedule for each six weeks available for teachers at your information station. Teachers can double-check their times and projects and also see if there are open slots when their students are running behind on a project.

- **Computer Maintenance Request Clipboard:** Here teachers can inform the technology specialist, or person in charge, of computer problems. Maybe they need software installed or a printer is malfunctioning. In that case, you may be able to fix the problem before or after school. If it is a more serious problem, you can contact the necessary county or district technicians to help solve the problem.

- **Software Inventory Clipboard:** It is nice to have this available to all so they can be sure they have the proper licensed software loaded on their computers. It is also a good idea to have more than one person responsible for software. For example, if the third grade teachers use some of their instructional budget to purchase software, they need access to the inventory sheets, as well.

BINDERS

- **Technology Lesson Plan Binder:** This is a great way to organize teaching ideas for a technology lab. Whether one person is responsible for these ideas or the whole school contributes activities, it is a fantastic way to offer integration ideas to teachers looking for ways to enrich their classroom learning. It is recommended that you organize these by subject area (language arts, math, social studies, etc.). This will allow third grade teachers to find good lessons from sixth grade teachers and then modify them to fit their own curriculum and skill level needs. Encourage your teachers to add to the Technology Lesson Plan Binder each time they have a new idea. Your school resources will continue to grow and change as technology education changes.

- **Software Help Binder:** Teachers always need quick and easy software tips. Because the day is so full, no one has time to weed through a software manual to have one simple question answered. However, when the lab manager has other responsibilities, he or she may not always be available to answer questions. Make FAQ (frequently asked questions) sheets for teachers' quick reference. It is an excellent idea if you are in charge of staff development for your teachers. Each time you do a staff development activity with your teachers or teach them a new skill, put the handouts you create in the binder. Now, teachers will always have access to that information.

- **Software Licensing Binder:** This will help keep track of software licensing. Use your Software Inventory Clipboard to keep track of what is currently loaded. You also need to keep up with the actual licenses for single-user packages, network licenses, lab packs, and site licenses.

- **Lab Information Binder:** What an important resource for a lab! This is a crucial component of an organized lab. However, you may want to keep it out of the reach of students. Based on your situation, these categories may or may not apply. There may be others that need to be included for your technology lab. This is just a suggested outline.

MANAGEMENT *(cont.)*

BINDERS (cont.)

1. Scheduling Information (how scheduling is done in the lab, time slots available, down/maintenance time, etc.)

2. Lab Software (what titles are available on which computers, station information, etc.)

3. Lab Hardware (information about computers, printers, scanners, etc.) This is a very important category. It can help you keep track of what systems need upgrades and how they were purchased (local money, county money, PTA, donations, etc.).

4. County Software (If your county or district makes county-purchased software available to you for review for possible purchase, keep track of what is new.)

5. System Information (important network information—how computers on the network are named, backup information, passwords, etc.) **Note:** Many people are hesitant to record passwords or to make them available to others. In some situations, as schoolwide technology infrastructures grow, there are so many different passwords, it can be difficult to keep track of all of them. What if the person responsible for the system is unreachable and there is a minor problem? The system information and necessary passwords need to be available.

6. School Technology Plan

7. County/District Technology Plan

- **Examples File Binder:** Designate a special area, maybe a filing cabinet or a bookcase, to contain exemplary student projects. Sharing successful student projects is an excellent way to promote student interest and set expectations. Arrange a filing system (may be arranged in the same way the Technology Lesson Plan Binder is organized) so that the teacher directing the activity can quickly access good student examples. Within this file, put a disk box. Purchase some extra disks on which to put examples of student slide shows and *HyperStudio* stacks for any type of project that is not printed. Each time you see a great project, save it onto one of these disks. Then, when introducing a new activity, you have a variety of student work from which to choose. It makes it much easier for students to visualize the outcome and, quite often, will raise student expectations.

MANAGEMENT *(cont.)*

BEHAVIOR HINTS

Quite often teachers find that students are on their very best behavior in the computer lab. Even those students who are often bouncing off the walls are so enthralled by technology that they actually stay planted for a 40-minute lesson.

However, without explicit expectations, any situation can become chaotic. And with expensive equipment around, the teacher cannot allow things to get out of control.

Allow whispering . . .

Students can (and will) quite often answer one another's questions if they are allowed to. While a "no tolerance" rule for talking seems to some like a way to keep students productive, it can also have the opposite effect.

. . . but control the noise level.

Allowing students to whisper sounds great in theory, but 20–30 students can create a lot of noise, even when working diligently on a project. If controlling noise is a priority, keep an egg timer handy. If the noise level climbs above normal, the whisper privilege is revoked for a short period of time. Set the egg timer for three to four minutes (any longer may result in lots of student questions and not enough teachers to answer them). Students are not allowed to talk until the buzzer sounds. This will both bring the noise level back down and remind students of the importance of being able to communicate with one another.

Look, no hands!

In a classroom, students are sometimes required to raise their hands to ask a question. But in the computer lab, that takes away valuable time on the keyboard when they could be answering their own questions. Many student questions in the computer lab involve specific software operations (e.g., how to delete a word, how to make a picture larger, etc.). If a student's hand is in the air, not only are his ot her own problem-solving capabilities taken away, but whatever the student next to him or her is doing becomes interesting, and a chain reaction of off-task behavior is likely to follow.

Bypass that problem by using cups to request attention. Place disposable cups next to each computer. If a student has a question, he or she places the cup on top of the computer monitor to signal the teacher that help is needed. If the student is able to answer his or her own question before the teacher arrives, the cup is returned to the side of the computer.

In a team-teaching situation with a professional in the computer lab and the classroom teacher attending with his or her class, a signal should be developed to differentiate between software questions and lesson questions. If a student has a technical or computer question about how to use a particular tool, place the cup upside down on the computer. If it is a content-related question about what was covered in the classroom, a student can signal the classroom teacher with the cup facing up.

MANAGEMENT *(cont.)*

THE MINI-LESSON

Those who have been forced to sit through a computer course where the instructor talked forever before allowing anyone to practice the things being demonstrated will support the mini-lesson. There is so much for students to learn about technology, and teachers want to share it all with them. However, as tool after tool after neat trick is introduced, explained and disssected, students begin to tune out. The happy medium for communicating enough information without frustrating students seems to be around five minutes. Start each and every activity with a mini-lesson. When students are learning a new piece of software, don't inundate them with every feature of the software.

On the other hand, when students already know a piece of software, teachers tend to say, "Go on and get started" without reviewing the program. Even if the lesson only involves changing a font or making a picture more spectacular, a teacher can provide students with one more tool to make their work the best it can be. Take about three to five minutes each day to share or, better yet, let a knowledgeable student share a valuable idea on the computer.

MANAGEMENT *(cont.)*

MINI-LESSON EXAMPLES:

Mrs. Loeber's class is typing a Civil War newsletter on the computer. It will take about four visits of 40 minutes each to the computer lab to type in the information, add graphics, edit, do the necessary formatting, and print. Instead of taking 20 minutes at the beginning of the first session to overwhelm students with how to type, change font and style, add pictures, edit, etc., she spends about four minutes at the beginning of each session to show them the tools that will help them get that day's objective met.

Day 1 Mini-Lesson (three minutes)

She reminds her students how to create a document and set its margins.

Her students spend the day typing in their information.

Day 2 Mini-Lesson (three to four minutes)

She shows (or reminds) her students how to change the font and size of the letters for headlines. Then she shows them how to change the text justification to centered where necessary and justified for the articles.

She goes over anything that her students struggled with on day one.

Day 3 Mini-Lesson (four to five minutes)

She shows her students how to import pictures into their documents, resize them, and wrap text.

She goes over anything that her students struggled with on day two.

Day 4 Mini-Lesson (three to five minutes)

She reminds her students of how to do final editing (use the Student Editing Checklist, if desired). She also shows them spell checker functions and how to catch common mistakes.

Students will retain more because they will have had the opportunity to apply what they learned each day.

Keep it short and sweet.

It is difficult to stop talking after only three to five minutes. The first time Mrs. Loeber tried to do this, she thought she did a great job and that her lesson was quick—it ended up lasting 15 minutes (and, of course, her students only retained half of what they heard). Practice keeping it short. Keep an egg timer handy to curtail any long-winded explanations. Tomorrow is another day, after all.

MANAGEMENT *(cont.)*

RULES

Have specific behavior expectations for students in the computer lab. Because the computer lab is different from the classroom, you may want to set specific guidelines for student behavior. As you introduce these rules, show the students exactly what it looks like if a student is following a rule and discuss examples of what might constitute breaking a rule. Use a role-playing exercise, if necessary, to demonstrate acceptable behavior.

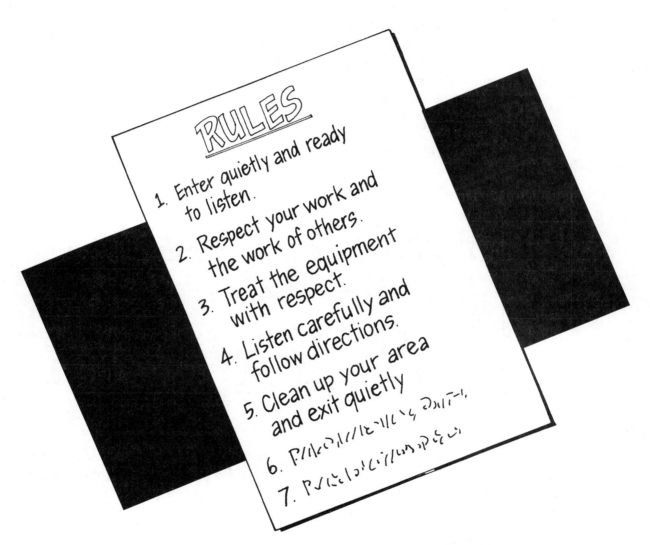

RULES
1. Enter quietly and ready to listen.
2. Respect your work and the work of others.
3. Treat the equipment with respect.
4. Listen carefully and follow directions.
5. Clean up your area and exit quietly

Set up very clear consequences for breaking the rules and be consistent.

THE ONE-COMPUTER CLASSROOM

Managing a classroom of 25 or more students is a challenge, even without introducing a computer. While it is an advantage and a privilege to have a computer in the classroom, hearing students complain "Sam got to work on the computer longer than me," or "I never get time on the computer" may make it seem like a burden. Changing the way the computer is managed in the classroom comes from changing the way it is used. The secret is to tap into the potential of the computer in the classroom and use it in many ways. Depending on the primary use of the computer, different scheduling methods will present themselves. If the computer is used as a free-time activity where students play games, scheduling is not much of an issue. However, if the computer is integrated into the curriculum, students will be responsible for producing technology projects; therefore, they must have larger blocks of equitable time on the computer. Look at the scheduling methods on the following pages.

Traditional Classroom Model

Integrated Classroom Model

SCHEDULING

ASSIGNED TIME

Depending on how the classroom is structured, this may or may not be a viable option. If the day is structured in small subject blocks (e.g., 40 minutes for math, 50 minutes for language arts, 30 minutes for physical education, 40 minutes for science), each with a whole-group lesson, practice, and a closure activity (or some similar arrangement), another method may be preferable. In this type of situation, a student assigned to the computer would be missing a whole-group activity and the work that accompanies it. Also, the time spent on the computer is very limited; the student is not able to make much progress in a five-minute trip to the computer.

However, if there is an integrated schedule with larger, thematic blocks (e.g., 120 minutes for a thematic block, 70 minutes for a writers' workshop, 60 minutes for math menus, etc.), assigned time might be very appealing. (See the sample daily schedule on pages 34 and 35. This method works in an integrated schedule because the large blocks of time usually consist of many different small-group activities taking place in the classroom while the teacher acts as a facilitator or "guide on the side." Because each unit/topic being studied in class contains a technology component, students know what is required of them during their computer time—work, not play.

When assigning students to a block of time, group them in mixed ability groups. They can choose a name, or a color code may be assigned to them (blue group, yellow group, etc.). For example, if the purple group is on the computer during the math block, the four to five students in the group may work on the computer during that time. During each week or each unit, every group should have computer time during every block. For some units, the technology component may be a group activity so all students in the group are contributing. When individual activities are assigned, students take turns at the computer, based on who is prepared and ready for the technology activity. This method may sound like a scheduling nightmare, but it is surprising how easily students are able to adjust once a routine is set.

MIXED ABILITY GROUPS

Blue Group	Yellow Group	Red Group	Purple Group	Green Group
BOB	AUSTIN	DARYL	RENEE	JOHN
DAWN	GEORGE	DIANE	KIMBERLY	JILL
KYLE	MIKE	BILL	JASON	ERIN
BARBARA	BYRON	PAMELA	GARY	DOREEN
MANUEL	JOE	CAROL	JUAN	TERESA

SCHEDULING *(cont.)*

SAMPLE DAILY SCHEDULE

	Monday	**Tuesday**
Opening Session 8:30–9:00	Monday Map Challenge: Asia (See the Mind Twisters on page 44.)	Tuesday Teaser—calculator decoding
Math Menus 9:00–10:00	Introduce weekly math menus—Do an introductory whole-group lesson on probability; see page 123.	Students work on their math menus; hold a math progress conference with the blue and yellow groups.
Special Area Class 10:00–10:40	Art	Music
Lunch 11:50–12:20		
Silent Reading 12:20–12:50		
Writer's Workshop 10:40–11:50	Open with the status of the class. Tall Tale—continue the writing process for the tall tale. Skills notebook—write compound sentences. The blue group works on the computer.	Open with the status of the class. Tall Tale—continue the writing process for the tall tale. Skills notebook—practice placing commas in compound sentences. Do peer editing. The red group works on the computer.
Thematic Unit 12:50–2:20	Continue the flight unit—flight vocabulary review; continue experiments on variables of flight; research flight history; highlight flight in WWII. Technology component—plan a slide show on flight. The green group works on the computer. Flight unit—begin designing and building balsa wood airplanes.	Continue working on flight history research paper. Highlight air safety. Technology component— prepare a slide show on flight. The yellow group works on the computer.
Language Arts/Writer's Workshop 2:20–3:00	Spotlight exaggeration in tall tales. Read *Paul Bunyan* in the anthology, pages 223–225. Find humorous exaggeration phrases. Have teacher-student conferencing. Study spelling.	Locate similes and metaphors in tall tales. Read aloud *John Henry*. Students take notes on similes and metaphors. Hold a writer's workshop on comparative writing. Hold a spelling conference.
Daily Closure 3:00–3:20	*Reminder: The tall tale rough draft must be conferenced by Thursday.	

SCHEDULING *(cont.)*

SAMPLE DAILY SCHEDULE

Wednesday	Thursday	Friday
Students work on math menus. Hold a math progress conference with the red and green groups.	Students work on math menus. Hold a math progress conference with the purple group.	Math menus closure—check on math progress; check up on probability.
Spanish	Technology/Video Production	P.E.
Open with the status of the class. Tall tale—continue the writing process for tall tale. Skills notebook—work on correcting run-on sentences. The yellow group works on the computer. Spotlight revision.	Open with the status of the class tall tale—continue the writing process for tall tale. Skills notebook—work on complex sentences. The green group works on the computer.	Hold a writing conference—tall tale draft—continue writing, share drafts, and engage in peer editing. The purple group works on the computer.
Flight unit—continue airplane design. Continue working on the flight history research paper. Highlight the biological effects of flying. Technology component—prepare a slide show on flight. The yellow group works on the computer.	Flight unit—continue the airplane design. Edit the flight history research paper. Highlight becoming a pilot/flight school. Technology component—prepare a slide show on flight. The purple group works on the computer.	Flight unit—the final copy of the flight research paper is due. Share blueprints for planes. Begin construction. The red group works on the computer.
	**Tomorrow, bring in materials for an airplane model.	

SCHEDULING *(cont.)*

To keep track of whose group is scheduled for computer time during the day, use a paper clip to hang a string from the ceiling over the computer. At each block changeover, hang the coordinating color of construction paper over the technology center. This signals the group that at some point during the small-group activities, they may work on the computer.

Hint: Make a daily helper the technology manager. This person will be in charge of changing the group assignment clip at the computer to alert the group to their computer time.

Sample Schedule:

Block	Monday	Tuesday	Wednesday	Thursday	Friday
Math	Purple	Blue	Red	Yellow	Green
Writer's Workshop	Blue	Red	Yellow	Green	Purple
Thematic Unit	Green	Yellow	Blue	Purple	Red
Language Arts	Yellow	Green	Purple	Red	Blue

EQUITY

Making sure all the students have the opportunity to work on the computer can be very difficult, but there are ways to make it easier to manage for teachers and students. Choose a visual way to display who has and has not been to the computer. Regardless of how student time on the computer is scheduled, this is a successful way to make sure one person is not monopolizing the computer.

The methods on the following pages allow the teacher and the students to do a quick scan to see who has had a recent turn on the computer and who still needs the opportunity.

Craft Sticks

Materials: marker, craft stick for every student, two jars/cups

Put each student's name on a craft stick. Label one jar "not yet" and one jar "been there." At the beginning of the week or unit, all students start out in the "not yet" jar. Once they have had turns on the computer, they must put their craft sticks in the "been there" jar. This does not mean they cannot use a computer a second time. Whenever the computer is available, it is fair game. However, it does mean that students in the "not yet" jar can bump a student off the computer who has already "been there."

SCHEDULING *(cont.)*

Clothespins

Materials: poster board (one piece), one clothespin for each student

Put each student's name on a clothespin. Draw a line down the middle of the poster board. The left side is reserved for students who have not been to the computer; the right side is for those who have been. Once they have had a turn on the computer, they move their clothespins to the other side. On this side could be listed alternative independent activities once each student has worked on a computer (writer's workshop, reading corner, research, puzzle center, etc.).

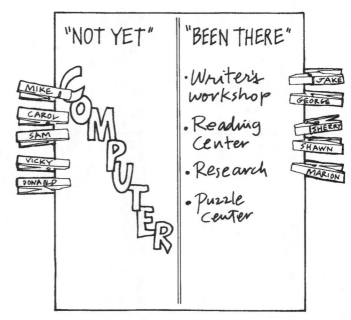

SIGN-UP SHEET

It may be desirable to use some blocks of time during your day as priority-based computer time. To use this time, students must sign up to work on a particular project and justify why they need the computer time. For example, if a student's project crashes or if a student is absent, that student may need extra computer time, as compared to a student who just wants to add some animation or play a problem-solving game for fun. The order and the amount of time that each student will have to work on a computer could be determined by need. This block of time could be first thing in the morning, during silent reading time, or some other consistent block of time during the day. Keep a sign-up sheet for each week on a clipboard near the technology center. There is a sign-up sheet on page 38 or make your own.

CLASSROOM MEETING

Hold a class meeting to get scheduling suggestions from your students. Share some different scheduling possibilities with them and ask them to share their thoughts and ideas. Students have wonderful, creative ideas to offer and can provide novel solutions to common, frustrating situations. Additionally, the majority of students often find it easier to follow rules and schedules that they have had a part in creating.

It is unlikely that any one of these methods alone will solve all of the scheduling problems a teacher faces. Try a combination of these methods, or create a custom scheduling variation. Because all classrooms are unique, their scheduling needs are, as well. The important thing is to not let your computer sit idle, waiting to be utilized.

SCHEDULING *(cont.)*

COMPUTER SIGN-UP SHEET

WEEK OF _____

Students: Be sure to fill in your name, project, reason you need to work on it, and the time needed to finish it. If any of these columns are left blank, your request will not be considered. Leave the Scheduled Time column blank so you can be assigned a time.

Student Name	Project	Reason	Time Needed	Scheduled Time

PLANNING

Planning for the one-computer classroom requires a different mind set from that for a whole-group situation. Instead of being used with a whole-class activity, generally the classroom computer is used by an individual or a small group. Although many of the same activities may be used, the activities need to be structured somewhat differently.

SUGGESTIONS FOR USING THE LESSON PLANS IN THIS BOOK

These lesson plan ideas are meant to be applicable in a variety of situations—the lab, the mini-lab, and even with a single classroom computer. However, with only one computer, some parts of each lesson plan will need to be structured differently than for a classroom full of computers. Because many of the activities in this book require planning in advance, students will be ready to go to the computer at different times. Try using the scheduling methods recommended in the preceding section and the management recommendations below to make each activity work in a one-computer classroom.

1. When time is limited yet the project is well suited to the unit, allow students to work in small groups or pairs to complete their projects. Make sure one student is not monopolizing the computer time by using a "keyboard" egg timer. (For example, two students are working together. The egg timer is set for five minutes, and one of the students has control of the keyboard for the first five minutes. When the first five minutes is up, the keyboard responsibility goes to the second student and the timer is reset.) At the end of the project, have each student write a paragraph telling how they each have contributed to the overall success of their project.

2. Introduce the activity to the entire class. Explain the objectives of the lesson and the expectations. Develop a time line for the unit and allow students to work on the project individually. Be sure to have project directions clearly posted at the computer workstation and a Software Hints Sheet for the specific program being used. This allows each student to work independently without interrupting the teacher during other small-group activities.

3. Occasionally, students will need extra help on the computer. Designate a technology team for the classroom. This can be per project, per software package, or per semester. The technology team should be a list of students who are accessible to any student having problems on a computer. Train these students how to answer questions, how to demonstrate or explain the answer to the student, and how NOT to solve the problem for the student.

4. Keep up with student progress by using a Status of the Class Management Sheet (page 41). This helps track who is using their time wisely and who may be struggling with the activity.

5. Have student-teacher technology conferences. Allow students to have one-on-one time with the teacher to show off their projects. This allows the teacher to keep close track of progress and achievement.

PLANNING *(cont.)*

INTEGRATING INSTRUCTIONAL SOFTWARE INTO THE CLASSROOM

Instructional software has its own unique niche in the one-computer classroom. Many teachers are familiar with instructional games but do not see their value. When integrated correctly into the curriculum, instructional software can offer a valuable extension to classroom learning or critical practice for those who need it.

Some instructional software can provide experiences and feedback to students during individual practice time that no worksheet or math page can do. This can be especially valuable for the student who needs the extra reinforcement.

Search for software that offers a variety of experiences and activities, from drill and practice to simulation and on to synthesis. For example, when searching for math software, find a program that questions students in different ways, not a package that just asks them to fill in the blanks. Also, many software packages are too level specific. Check to make sure the activities reach students at a variety of levels.

There are some simulation software packages available that do an excellent job of making history, math, language arts, etc., more meaningful for students. Excellent examples of this are **MECC's Trail** packages. *The Oregon Trail*, *The Amazon Trail*, and *The Yukon Trail* put students in historically and geographically accurate situations and quite often get them emotionally involved. Students begin to value the decisions they make, whether they are solving a math problem integrated into the package or making critical decisions about which direction to travel.

These types of packages often require less planning and management than productivity activities that are done in the classroom. However, there are a number of misleading educational software packages on the market. Beware of the games that offer bells and whistles but little substance. Choose software carefully—it can end up being a big waste of money.

Hint: Most educational software dealers and companies offer demos or previews of software. It is well worth the effort to preview software.

PLANNING *(cont.)*

STATUS OF THE CLASS MANAGEMENT SHEET

Project: _____   **Project Dates:** _____

Student Name														

MANAGEMENT

One of the most important parts of technology management in the classroom is setting behavioral expectations. Many teachers feel they do not know as much about the computer as their students, so they do not give them a clear introduction to it and their expectations regarding its usage. Although many computer novices have a fear of harming the computer, many students have the opposite approach. They are almost hardened to the presence of technology due to their experiences with video games, computers, and other electronic equipment around the home and, therefore, do not treat the machines carefully. It is never too late to teach students how to treat a computer with respect and to reinforce that in the classroom.

At the beginning of the year as students are given a tour of their new classroom, introduce the computer. Set up rules as a class about what can and cannot be done to and at the computer. If possible, come up with a short set of expectations about computer usage as a class and post them at the computer. If students are responsible for coming up with the rules, they tend to take ownership of them and their enforcement.

Some Example Rules

1. Be kind to the equipment.

2. Eating and drinking should be done away from the computer.

3. Respect the work of others.

Even where teachers have very open classrooms, mistreatment of classroom equipment should not be tolerated and should result immediately in loss of computer time. The life of a computer is very often shortened by the way it is treated, and it will spend time gathering dust in the back of the room if it is not working correctly. Avoid this situation by educating your students from the beginning and give them the responsibility to care properly for their classroom computers.

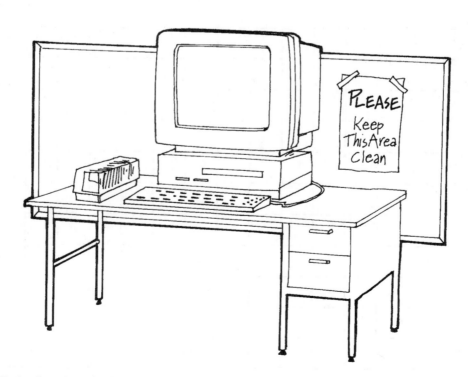

MANAGEMENT *(cont.)*

INTRODUCING STUDENTS TO HARDWARE

If a teacher has been trained in how to take the computer apart, students can be shown what the inside looks like. (Students should not try this at home.) Show them the power source and compare it to a light bulb that becomes hotter the longer it is on. This is a good time to explain why food and drink are not permitted around a computer. It is also a good time to talk about the cooling system of a computer (the fan and vents). Explain to them how the vents need to be exposed to allow air to flow in order to keep the computer cool. Show them the delicate workings of the disk drive. Explain why nothing except a computer disk should ever go into the disk drive. In fact, if students do not use disks, the disk drive may be covered with a piece of construction paper. The drive can be ruined due to the dust and chalk in the air if not properly cared for. (Try not to make any permanent, drastic modifications to the computer—such as removing the disk or hard drive—since it is likely to be passed on to another teacher.)

Explain to students how they should care for floppy disks. (1) They should never pull the protective covering away from a disk and then try to touch the disk itself. Touching the actual disk can damage it and destroy all of the work saved on it. (2) Put the disk in its protective envelope or a carrying case before transporting it anywhere. (3) Never place a disk near a magnet; it could erase whatever is on it forever.

If the computer has a CD-ROM player, show students how to change the compact discs (CDs). Students in grades three to five should be able to handle this task, but if they mistreat the CDs, designate a few responsible students in the classroom to handle this responsibility.

Discuss the treatment of the cords, keyboard, and mouse. Set expectations about what to do if they become disconnected. Upper grade teachers can train a small group of students about the setup of a computer; primary and middle grades may want to handle this situation themselves or inform their technology specialist. However, some students, no matter what their grade level, know a great deal about computer maintenance.

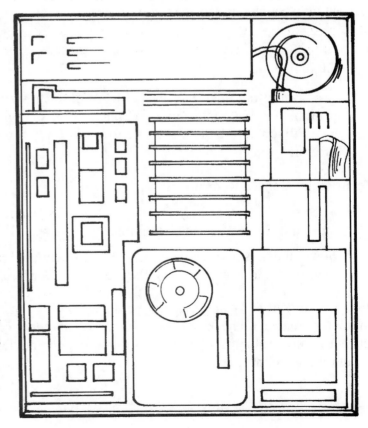

It is very important to teach students the proper way to treat a computer and inform them that no mistreatment of the classroom computer will be tolerated. It isn't necessary to make students afraid of the computer to do this; just make them aware. Once the mystery of the computer has been taken away, students will have more respect for the computer and help the classroom community obey the rules.

MANAGEMENT *(cont.)*

THE CLASSROOM COMPUTER: A TECHNOLOGY CENTER

The classroom computer should not be just a machine in the corner but a center of productivity. Do not treat the computer as a piece of furniture but put some real thought into its role in the classroom environment.

Technology Center Placement

- If at all possible, try to face the computer monitor towards a wall. This will reduce the distraction the computer causes for other students in class.

- Try to avoid placing the classroom computer next to a chalkboard or a pencil sharpener. Both of these create dust that can damage the computer's disk drive.

- Try to locate the computer in a place where it can be used as a demonstration station. There will be situations when the computer can be utilized for group demonstrations. Placement near an overhead (if an LCD panel [liquid crystal display panel]) or television (if you have an LTV card or an AV machine), if available, can be very helpful for use with the whole classroom.

Technology Center Materials

- Some schools have become so technology infused that computer disks are as much a part of the student supply list as pencils and paper. Have students bring in computer disks to use throughout the year for special projects. Disks can be bought very cheaply if purchased in bulk. Have students bring in money (a fraction of the cost of buying them separately), use part of the instructional budget, or team up with other interested teachers to order disks from a supply catalog at a discounted bulk rate.

- Purchase a clip attachment for the computer to provide students a place to clip their rough drafts or multimedia planning sheets. These can be purchased for under $10 at most computer or office supply stores.

- If a printer (dot matrix) is available, offer a variety of types of ribbons. Use a black ribbon for printing text only and save those fancy color ribbons for printing things with pizzazz. There are even ribbons available that make iron-ons for T-shirts. Have colored paper available for special printing projects.

Technology Center References

- Keep the Software Shortcuts, pages 149–158, available for students. It will help them become more independent on the computer.

- Make manuals and computer trade books available to students. They will use them to answer their own questions; besides, they are great technical reading.

Assign a student daily or weekly to be the technology manager. This student can help keep the computer area neat, check to make sure the computer is on or off and working properly, alert the teacher to any problems, change the group assignment clip, and do anything else necessary to help maintain the technology center.

THE MULTI-COMPUTER CLASSROOM

Having multiple computers in a classroom provides more opportunities to truly integrate technology into teaching. The multi-computer classroom is usually considered when three or more computers are available for student use (scheduling, planning, and management for the two-computer classroom is probably more similar to the one-computer classroom). Having several computers in your classroom allows you to engage small groups of students (up to the entire class) in technology activities. It also allows you to use the computer in many different ways simultaneously (e.g., as a math center, as a writing tool, in a science experiment, etc.).

SCHEDULING

Scheduling time for students to work on the computer will always be an issue. There are many methods suggested for the one-computer classroom that will also work in the multi-computer classroom. However, differences do exist.

Scheduling the day in long, thematic blocks (pages 34 and 35) is probably the best way to utilize the computers in a mini-lab setting. It allows you to have students working on technology all day so the computers never sit idle. However, students and activities still need to be arranged carefully to best utilize the time.

ASSIGNED TIME

Assign students to a computer. If there are five computers in your classroom and 25 students, a group of five students would be assigned to each computer. These students create their projects on this computer, publish writing here, and engage in instructional activities. This makes management somewhat easier because only five students are scheduled per computer instead of 25. Make each student group as much of a mixture as possible; combine students with different abilities (academic and social), genders, and technology competency levels in each group. The students will be able to learn from one another and use the strengths and individual talents that they bring to the group. Switch your groups every 6–12 weeks to give the students the opportunity to work with everyone in the class.

PLANNING

The lessons in this book work well in the multi-computer classroom. The main issue is scheduling the time for your students to do their work. When creating technology projects, try to create projects that lend themselves to cooperative group activities. For example, create a project (or modify a lesson in this book) so that it has specific jobs. Each day, students are assigned the jobs they will perform during that day's cooperative technology experience. Have students use the Job Performance Record (page 48) to keep track of their contributions to the group.

MANAGEMENT

In any classroom, there are certain behavioral expectations. A teacher's expectations will not be any different in a multi-computer classroom than in a classroom with one computer. For student management suggestions, refer to the section on the one-computer classroom (pages 42–44).

Use Cooperative Learning Groups

Organize the students into cooperative learning groups so they can get the most out of computer time. Keep in mind that this is different from putting students in a group and telling them to share their work. Effective cooperative learning requires prior planning and adequate management by the teacher. It also takes effort and self-control on the part of the students. There are available to teachers many resources that give the whats, hows, and whys of cooperative learning. Refer to these to help make cooperative learning work for you. (For example, TCM 651, 654, 657, and 660: Cooperative Learning Activities for Language Arts, Social Studies, Math, and Science)

Example of Cooperative Learning and Technology

The Inventors and Inventions project

Students are assigned the following jobs which change from day to day.

Day Two

(On day one, your students worked as a group to select their inventor and made a plan to complete the project.)

Researcher: This person is responsible for finding information and helpful resources to aid in the research of the inventor. This may include using a computer to research via the Internet or CD-ROMs, or it may include going to the school media center to find resources. The student takes notes on the Inventor Research Sheet. On this day, the student is required to find information about the inventor's early life.

Researcher

MANAGEMENT *(cont.)*

Graphics Manager: This student searches for helpful pictures, diagrams, artwork, and even animations or video clips for the project. This may include scanning pictures, using the Internet to download graphics, or finding helpful pictures via CD-ROM. This person can also work with the researcher to find good resources.

Graphics Manager

Computer Engineers: This pair of students shares the responsibility of working on the actual *HyperStudio* stack (setting up or working on the frame of the stack, adding effects, typing in information). To balance time evenly between the two computer engineers, use an egg timer to measure keyboard time. (Every five to ten minutes have students switch.) The student who is "off" the computer acts as an encourager and organizer for the student using the keyboard.

Hints for Using Cooperative Learning with Technology

Do not expect students to be able to work well in cooperative groups if they have not

Computer Engineers

done so before. It takes very good organization and management, as well as practice. Do not give up on it if the first experience does not go smoothly. Learn from mistakes, make changes, talk to the students, and give it a second chance.

Use checklists and rubrics to keep students accountable for their share of the work. One of the main challenges with cooperative learning is training students to do their portion of the work and putting in place the checks and balances that will keep students on track. Use a popular cooperative learning checklist or the Job Performance Record on page 48 to manage your students' participation.

Allow for Individual Projects

Cooperative learning helps to keep students involved at all times on projects, but not all projects lend themselves to cooperative group organization. Allow students to do their own individual projects where they are the only ones accountable. This gives them the opportunity to test their own technology skills and evaluate their own proficiency rather than that of a group's.

MANAGEMENT *(cont.)*

Name: _____

Project: _____

Job Performance Record

Keep track of the duties you perform in your group each day you work on your project. Have the other students in your group initial each day to verify that you fulfilled your responsibilities.

Day # _____
Date: _____
Job: _____
The things I contributed to my group today were

_____

_____

Student Initials: _____

Day # _____
Date: _____
Job: _____
The things I contributed to my group today were

_____

_____

Student Initials: _____

Day # _____
Date: _____
Job: _____
The things I contributed to my group today were

_____

_____

Student Initials: _____

Day # _____
Date: _____
Job: _____
The things I contributed to my group today were

_____

_____

Student Initials: _____

ASSESSMENT: MAKING IT WORK WITH TECHNOLOGY

Once a teacher is ready to start integrating technology into the classroom, how does he or she assess student achievement? Creating multimedia projects and other technology related activities requires a variety of skills. The methods of assessing students in all areas is changing, and technology projects are an excellent place to start using alternative assessments. Students are no longer evaluated solely by paper-and-pencil tests where there is one correct answer. Students are now required to use their diverse abilities and skills to construct their own responses.

Definition of Assessment:

Assessment is the collection of data or gathering of information regarding one's progress.

PERFORMANCE-BASED ASSESSMENTS

There are all types of assessments that work well with technology. Student performance can be evaluated with a checklist, a rubric, or even an anecdotal record. These types of assessments not only give the student information about how he or she did on a particular project but also provide him or her with specific information about the areas that require the most improvement.

Many teachers are finding that with technology projects, they need to look closely at the process, not just the product. A technology project may be the culmination of an entire unit, encompassing over a month's worth of student work and many different types of skills. How does one evaluate that kind of effort from students?

To devise the assessment of a project, it is much easier if a project is broken down into manageable parts. These should match the educational objectives of the project.

Think about what is to be evaluated.

Examples for a *ClairsWorks* slide show:

Prior Planning: Did the student complete the planning sheet required?

Use of Technology Tools: Was the student able to use the hardware and software effectively?

Student Research (the content): Did the student provide the required content for the project?

Creativity or Imagination: Did the student take any creative risks?

Grammar/Technical Skills: Did the student meet the requirements for grammar and mathematics?

ASSESSING STUDENT PRODUCTS

SHARE THE PLAN

When creating a student project, up-front initial student involvement is the key to students taking ownership of the project. While preparing to start a new unit, tell them about the technology component. Allow them to start thinking about it before the content of the unit is even introduced. It will encourage students to be accountable for the content necessary to complete the project.

DISCUSS YOUR GOALS

After introductory lessons in the unit, talk to students about what they think should be included in the project. What should be required? What should be evaluated?

SHARE THE ASSESSMENT

Put the assessment in terms they understand. Use their words. Try to stay away from teacher jargon; if it is used, students may not know whether they have met the objective or not. Let them help to determine exactly what is required. If they know this from the beginning, they will be more likely to meet a teacher's expectations.

There are sample assessments scattered throughout this book. Because every classroom is different, the assessment that is most effective is the one which is specifically created with students. Individualize the sample assessments as guides to creating rubrics and checklists for classroom use.

SELF-ASSESSMENT

Help students learn how to use self-assessments as tools to improve their work. Students very often struggle with organization. Using a self-assessment to help them evaluate their performance on a project as they do it can assist them in achieving the quality they desire.

ASSESSING STUDENT PRODUCTS *(cont.)*

ASSESSMENT EXAMPLE: EXPLORERS

As the explorer unit begins, the teacher gives the students the plan for the unit.

Teacher: "Through literature and research over the next six weeks, we are going to discover why and how people explored. What motivated them to go out into the unknown? We will take a look at how they contributed to our society today through their discoveries. You will also have an individual project. Each student will research an explorer and create his or her own multimedia project, using either a *ClarisWorks* slide show or a *HyperStudio* stack about their chosen explorer. We will talk more about the project later. Now, let us learn about explorers."

After students begin to learn about explorers, the teacher can talk to them about their projects in more depth.

Teacher: "Okay, now that we have learned a little bit about explorers, let us recap what we have already learned and think about what we need to include in a project about an explorer. Any suggestions?"

Student: "How about when they lived and when they explored?"

Student: "How about what they were looking for?"

In the discussion that ensues, the teacher and students together can decide exactly what might be included in the project. It is important at this point to guide students toward the educational goals they have in mind for the project. List the requirements for the project on a piece of chart paper for all of the students to see. Keep this posted throughout the unit to keep students on track. Now begin discussing how to assess the project.

Teacher: "Let us talk about how we are going to tell if you are successful on this project. First, we need to look at what we have decided as a class to include in the project. What must each project have to be considered as meeting these goals?"

Student: "We need to tell about our explorer and when he lived. That is important. If that is not included, then the project is not complete."

Teacher: "Okay, our first evaluation criteria is to introduce our explorer and tell about when he lived."

Discuss with students all of the necessary components to the project and exactly what will be evaluated. Decide up front if grammar and spelling will be assessed. Decide if artwork or creativity is important. Ask students what they think should be emphasized. Come up with a list of things from students to evaluate. Tell students what you think is important to do in this project.

ASSESSING STUDENT PRODUCTS *(cont.)*

Create a rubric or checklist including the criteria that the teacher and the class have decided upon. The next day, share it with the class.

MULTIMEDIA PRESENTATION 5-POINT RUBRIC

	5	4	3	2	1	0
Overall Presentation	The project flows well, keeps the attention of the audience, and is very interesting.	Project flows well and is interesting.	Majority of project flows well and has some interesting items included.	Majority of project is disjointed and interest level is sporadic.	Project does not flow at all, is poorly presented, and has no interest whatsoever.	No response.
Text Information	The information used is accurate, well written, complete with proper grammar and punctuation.	Majority of the text is accurate, uses proper grammar and punctuation, and mostly flows well.	Uses an acceptable amount of text. Information is accurate. Acceptable grammar and punctuation.	Text information is short and inaccurate. Grammar and punctuation are mostly incorrect.	Information is missing, and grammar and punctuation is misused.	No response.
Graphics and Scanned Images	Images are used to enhance the information and support text. Placement of images is pleasing to the eye.	Images are used to enhance the information and support text. Placement of images is appropriate.	Images enhance the information somewhat. Placement of images is acceptable.	Images used have relevance to information. Not enough images used.	No graphics or scanned images used.	No response.

Teacher: "Yesterday we discussed what we were looking for in this upcoming social studies project. This is the assessment that I put together based on what we as a class decided is important."

Share the assessment.

Teacher: "Will this tool tell us if we did what we set out to do?"

Discuss any changes that may need to be made.

Teacher: "As we work on our projects over the next three weeks, doing the research and putting together our projects, refer to this assessment to stay on track. This is how your projects will be assessed."

This gives your students a choice, and it also gives them information that will guide them as they prepare for the project.

ASSESSING STUDENT PRODUCTS *(cont.)*

SELF-ASSESSMENT

Evaluate your performance on this project, using the following scale:

Not Yet = I did not meet the requirements.

Almost There = I was very close but fell short of meeting the requirements.

I Did It! = I met the requirements.

Above and Beyond = I went above and beyond what was required by doing something extra.

Explain why you earned that rating. Include evidence or reasons that demonstrate it.

1. I selected an appropriate topic.

   Not Yet　　　　　　　Almost There　　　　　I Did It!　　　　　Above and Beyond

   Why?_____

2. I did the required research or preparation.

   Not Yet　　　　　　　Almost There　　　　　I Did It!　　　　　Above and Beyond

   Why?_____

3. I was well prepared when it was time to work on the computer.

   Not Yet　　　　　　　Almost There　　　　　I Did It!　　　　　Above and Beyond

   Why?_____

4. My project has the required parts.

   Not Yet　　　　　　　Almost There　　　　　I Did It!　　　　　Above and Beyond

   Why?_____

5. I used creativity in my project.

   Not Yet　　　　　　　Almost There　　　　　I Did It!　　　　　Above and Beyond

   Why?_____

The best thing about my project is _____

I could improve my project if I _____

Things I learned doing this project were _____

I filled out this evaluation honestly.　　　　Yes ❏　　　　　No ❏

Signature _____

Date_____

ELECTRONIC PORTFOLIOS

One great way that technology can help teachers meet their educational goals is by helping them improve the way they assess student progress across the curriculum. Portfolios are already an excellent way to show what a student has achieved; they are not a single piece of information like a test score but a collection of representative student work samples gathered over time. Portfolios also allow the individuality of a student to appear throughout the different types of work included. If a student has a particular gift for writing and self-expression, or art perhaps, it can be much more evident in a portfolio than in a student performance on a test or worksheet.

Portfolios are a collection of student work showing where the student started, the progress the student has made, and a sense of what the student is capable of doing. Portfolios are becoming the overwhelming choice of school teachers because by including appropriate work samples, they show much more of what the student can do compared to a paper-and-pencil assessment. Portfolios can include things such as the following:

- **MY GOALS FOR THE YEAR**
- **A FAVORITE PIECE OF WRITING**
- **THE HARDEST MATH PROBLEM I CAN SOLVE**
- **MY NEATEST WORK**
- **THE MOST CHALLENGING PROJECT I HAVE COMPLETED**

Advantages of Electronic Portfolios over Traditional Assessment

- They provide examples of representational student work.
- They provide more information about the students' capabilities than a number or letter.
- They allow students to have more choices about their assessments, thereby causing them to be more motivated.
- They show changes and growth of student achievement over time.
- They encompass a wide variety of skills.
- They are an excellent communication tool for students to share their progress.
- They allow for student individuality.
- They help students develop skills in self-assessment.

Advantages of Electronic Portfolios over Traditional Portfolios

- Electronic portfolios do not take up as much classroom space (boxes, file cabinets full of student work, or sample projects). This makes it easy to add to the portfolio from year to year without its becoming too large and cumbersome.
- Working in electronic portfolios makes it easy to organize and manipulate.
- Electronic portfolios make it easy to scroll through the student samples to find pieces that are significant to the viewer.
- Electronic portfolios make it easy to include large projects (pictures and descriptions), video clips (performances and interviews), and recordings (readings, reflections, and songs). They offer a variety of media for self-expression.

ELECTRONIC PORTFOLIOS *(cont.)*

CREATING PORTFOLIOS

There are software packages designed specifically to help set up portfolios. Scholastic's *Electronic Portfolio* is an example of one of those packages. It comes with examples at every grade level, a template, and an excellent tutorial that leads the user through the process of creating his or her first portfolio. (Scholastic, (800) 325-6149)

Many teachers think that to create electronic portfolios for (or with) their students, they must purchase an extra piece of software with the one purpose of creating student portfolios. The good news is that there is popular software (possibly already on your computer) that can be used to do the same thing. Many teachers have created wonderful student portfolios with *HyperStudio*. There are also many teachers who have charged their students with the creations of their own portfolios, using these very programs. This reduces a teacher's work load and gives the students more freedom, responsibility, and control over their own portfolios.

The Bare Minimum:

> a computer
>
> *ClarisWorks* or *HyperStudio*

The Basics:

> a computer
>
> *ClarisWorks* or *HyperStudio*
>
> scanner

The Ultimate Electronic Portfolio Station:

> video camera
>
> multimedia computer w/video editing capabilities (e.g., AV Mac)
>
> digital camera
>
> color scanner
>
> *Electronic Portfolio* (Scholastic), *HyperStudio*, or *ClarisWorks*

STUDENT-CREATED PORTFOLIOS

Objective: To engage each student in a project to show how he or she has progressed from the beginning to the end of the school year.

Materials: *ClarisWorks* or *HyperStudio,* a digital camera (optional), a scanner (optional), a folder or shoebox in which to organize work, and a plan

Before beginning the year, decide what the purpose of the portfolio is and what components need to be included for it to achieve this purpose. Revisit what is important in student achievement. Look at the process of helping students become better thinkers, helping them recognize their own achievements, and deciding what should be included in the student portfolio.

ELECTRONIC PORTFOLIOS *(cont.)*

CLARISWORKS PORTFOLIO

Students collect samples of their work in the approved categories. These are organized in a file folder or shoebox. (If the projects are scanned and put on disk, the project itself can be sent home.)

Throughout the year each student creates slides to go in his or her portfolio slide show. These slides contain information about experiences they have had in the classroom and their personal goals. They can also create slides in reaction to a unit or their performance on a test or project. It is important to keep up with this portion of the project by having students create slides every four to six weeks. This will help show your students' progress from the first day to the last day of the school year.

At the end of the year each student creates a slide show containing the slides he or she created throughout the year, as well as new slides that explain his or her reactions to and feelings about his or her portfolio and why he or she selected the work he or she did. Digital pictures and scanned-in work can be included in the slide show, or the teacher or a parent viewing the portfolio can have the work samples handy while viewing each student's slide show.

Organizational tip: At the end of each unit, have students create slides about their learning experiences. Have one day a month to create "reflection" slides where each student reflects over his or her progress for that month.

HYPERSTUDIO PORTFOLIO

HyperStudio is an excellent piece of software to use in portfolio creation. *HyperStudio* allows you to easily import text and pictures, include sound, and make additions and changes. *HyperStudio* also makes it easy to include video clips and *QuickTime* movies.

Give students guidelines about the components of their portfolios. Use a menu at the beginning to allow parents or teachers to navigate through goals, work samples, anecdotal notes, and student projects. Give your students some creative freedom, but try to manage the important ingredients of the portfolio.

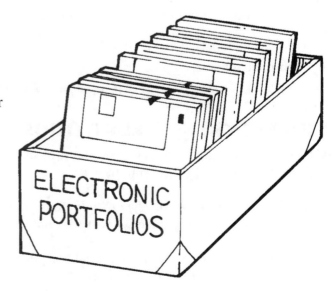

Try to have the portfolio completed (or at least ready to view) by the time final parent-teacher conferences are being held. Invite each student to share his or her portfolio with his or her parents and to explain what he or she learned throughout the process.

INTEGRATING THE INTERNET INTO THE CURRICULUM

WHAT IS THE INTERNET?

TELECOMMUNICATIONS

A discussion of the Internet cannot begin without understanding telecommunications. It is the ability for computers to exchange information over distance. This is usually done with a piece of hardware called a modem. Modems translate the digital information that a computer uses into analog, or sound information, that can be transmitted over telephone lines. Once transmitted, a computer equipped with a modem at the other end of the line receives the analog information and translates it back to its digital form. Computers can use this "connectivity" to exchange documents, programs, or mail and even control each other.

WHAT IS A NETWORK?

Today, "network" is trendy term, meaning to get together with other people to exchange ideas or information, was actually derived from the computer term "network." A computer network is two or more computers that are linked so that they can communicate with each other. Networks are usually "hard-wired," meaning they do not need modems to communicate. A local area network (LAN) is the connection of computers at a common site, like a school or business. These LANs can be attached to a wide area network (WAN). Many school districts have begun to attach their networks to the Internet.

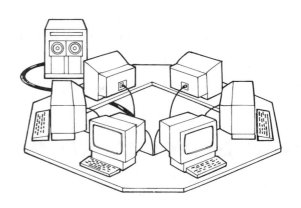

The Internet is the "network of networks." It is a global technology network made up of many smaller contributing networks. They all speak a common language called Internet protocol or IP. This system gives immediate access to information. It is like being able to open any book in any library from a computer. A teacher can look at and print articles, documents, and pictures, as well as review current facts about news, weather, and sports that may be used in the classroom. However, the Internet is not

merely a librarian; this tool also makes it possible for users to communicate through electronic mail (e-mail), in real time on chat lines, or even through video conferencing.

The Internet was created in 1983 with 100 networks and has grown by leaps and bounds. By 1993, there were approximately 10,000 networks attached to the Internet. Most experts believe the amount of networks currently attached to the Internet is in the hundreds of thousands. Since each of the connected networks can be as many as tens of thousands of computers, the number of individual users of the Internet is probably in the millions.

WHAT IS THE INTERNET? *(cont.)*

WHY USE THE INTERNET IN THE CLASSROOM?

The Internet gives teachers, parents, and students access to information of a quality and quantity never seen before in education. Using the Internet allows the user to retrieve information, media, and even software from all over the world. This allows studenTs, and teachers using this tool to have this valuable information for individual or cooperative projects.

But gathering information is merely one aspect of the power of the Internet—communication is the other. Once a teacher has access to the Internet, he or she has access to all the users of the Internet—teachers sharing and collaborating with other teachers, students with other students, scientists, and business people, everyone. Distance, class, race, and culture are no longer barriers to the sharing of ideas. People can simply communicate.

Some uses of the Internet include, but are not limited to, the following:

- gathering information on almost any subject
- communicating with others via e-mail
- joining discussion groups on a specific topic
- publishing student work
- communicating with experts in any field
- taking part in electronic expeditions

WHAT CAN YOU DO WITH THE INTERNET?

No, it won't make julienne fries, but if it's information and communication you want, a better question might be, "What can't the Internet do?" Most functions of the Internet fall into these following families:

- Electronic Mail (e-mail): Correspond electronically with people who are connected to the "Net."
- Usenet Newsgroups: A worldwide bulletin board service is divided into interests. You "post" messages and others "post" replies.
- Mailing Lists: These are e-mail lists that are divided by interests. You send e-mail to interest groups and they reply.
- TELNET: Log onto and use a computer from a remote location.
- File Transfer Protocol (FTP): Transfer files like software and documents from one computer to another.
- Internet Relay Chat (IRC): Engage in discussions with others simply by typing.
- World Wide Web (WWW): Gather information through the use of the new graphic information system.

Don't let this list scare you. In the past separate pieces of software and/or long strings of commands would have been needed to carry out any one of these functions. With today's Internet browsers, all of these functions can be done using one program, often transparently.

NETIQUETTE AND NETHICS

THE RULES OF THE INFORMATION SUPERHIGHWAY

Before getting started down the information superhighway, it is important to know the rules of the road.

From the *Concise Oxford Dictionary*:

Etiquette: n. conventional rules of personal behavior in polite society

Ethic[s]: n. 1. a. relating to morals, treating of moral questions; morally correct; honorable

Just as there are behaviors which are acceptable at school, students need to learn the correct procedures and rules for using the Internet. Netiquette, the etiquette of the Net, and nethics, the ethics of the Net, are the rules of the information superhighway.

You're Not Dealing with Computers; You're Dealing with People

When interacting with someone on the Internet, be careful of what is said. Writing has to be much clearer than oral conversation to avoid misinterpretation. Sending a message that is strongly critical is called a "flame." To avoid "flaming," never say anything to someone that wouldn't be said to them in person. Avoid the use of sarcasm and be careful with humor. Without voice inflections and body language, remarks are easily misinterpreted.

Do Not Post Personal Information About Anyone

The Internet is becoming a very crowded place. Like society as a whole, there are nice people and there are not-so-nice people. Never release personal information to anyone.

Be Brief

More people will read information only if it is short and clear.

Do Not Harass Users

Do not abuse the right to freedom of expression; others have the right to be free from harassment.

Be Careful of Copyrights

Cut and paste functions make electronic media extremely easy to use when communicating one's own, as well as others', ideas. As long as an article is used for educational purposes, it may be used. It is important, however, to cite all references.

Double-Check Downloads

There are many software products available on the Internet. Many of these products are offered free of charge. Be sure the software product being downloaded is not a commercial product that has been distributed illegally. Most commercial software products have a title screen with a copyright statement.

Give Credit Where Credit Is Due

Remember, the work that someone has placed on the Internet is free to use, but if used, give the author or creator credit.

NETIQUETTE AND NETHICS *(cont.)*

THE TEN COMMANDMENTS FOR COMPUTER ETHICS (NETHICS) FROM THE COMPUTER ETHICS INSTITUTE

1. Thou shalt not use a computer to harm other people.
2. Thou shalt not interfere with other people's computer work.
3. Thou shalt not snoop around in other people's files.
4. Thou shalt not use a computer to steal.
5. Thou shalt not use a computer to bear false witness.
6. Thou shalt not use or copy software for which you have not paid.
7. Thou shalt not use other people's computer resources without authorization.
8. Thou shalt not appropriate other people's intellectual output.
9. Thou shalt think about the social consequences of the program you write.
10. Thou shalt use a computer in ways that show consideration and respect.

SAFE SURFING

RULES FOR SAFE SURFING

Because the Internet is public domain, free speech is not only the right but the rule. Therefore, nearly anyone can publish almost anything on it. We must acknowledge the fact that there are inappropriate materials on the Internet and then do everything we can to actively avoid them. We cannot weed out all of the materials that are unacceptable for academic purposes, but it should be clearly understood by all students that access to such material in any form is strictly forbidden.

In order to make the responsibility of using this tool clear, many educational institutions have developed acceptable use plans or AUPs. These AUPs usually include a contract that is quite clear about the responsibilities of the student and must be signed by the student as well as their parents or guardians. To find examples of AUPs see the Armadillo WWW Server at:

http://www.rice.edu/armadillo/Rice/Resources/acceptable.html

Although the actual percentage of unacceptable materials is small, it is a cause for concern for students, parents, and teachers. If a student stumbles onto the information while doing legitimate research, he or she should contact the teacher or person responsible for technology at school.

There is no foolproof way of keeping students out of areas where they should not be. Here are a few general rules of thumb when students are surfing the Net:

- Supervise; keep an eye on students while they are using the Internet.
- Send an agreement home for parents to sign that explains benefits and risks of Internet research.
- Make students aware of "netiquette"—the rules of using the Internet.
- Take the time to teach students to be responsible Net citizens.
- Create a list of Internet sites that are safe. Require that your students visit only those areas.
- Create a home page with safe surfing links to safe and educationally sound Internet sites.
- Use one of the Net monitoring programs that are available to block out inappropriate information.
- Parents: Spend some family time Net surfing. There are plenty of sites that provide excellent material.

NET MONITORING SOFTWARE

Several products block inappropriate information from crossing the screens of minors. A few of the more popular are shown below. Limited time demos of each can be downloaded.

Cyber Patrol	http://www.cyberpatrol.com
Net Nanny	http://www.netnanny.com/
SurfWatch	http://www1.surfwatch.com/

GUIDELINES FOR PUBLISHING WORK ON THE INTERNET

The Internet can provide a global audience for students' work. There are several Internet sites listed in the back of this book that allow students to post projects. Before posting any student work, have a signed release from parents. A sample release is provided on the next page.

SAFE SURFING *(cont.)*

RELEASE FOR ELECTRONICALLY DISPLAYED STUDENT WORK

Dear Parents/Guardians,

We are excited to let you know that our class will be publishing our work on a portion of the Internet called the World Wide Web. This means that anyone in the world who has access to the Web will be able to view your child's work. The potential audience is in the millions.

Your signature below acknowledges permission for such work to be published on the World Wide Web.

Yours truly,

Classroom Teacher

☐ My child's work, which may be accompanied by his or her first name, may be electronically displayed and produced.

☐ My child's work, which may not be accompanied by his or her first name, may be electronically displayed and produced.

☐ Photographs of my child, which may be accompanied by his or her first name, may be electronically displayed and produced.

☐ Photographs of my child, which may not be accompanied by his or her first name, may be electronically displayed and produced.

I hereby give the above permission and release_____ from any liability resulting from or connected with the publication of such work.

_____
Child's Name

_____
Teacher

_____
Parent or Guardian Signature

_____
Date

CONNECTING TO THE INTERNET

WHAT DO I NEED TO GET CONNECTED?

Other than a computer there are only a couple of things that are needed to connect to the Internet.

Modem

Computers speak and understand digital language. Telephone lines carry what is called analog information. A modem facilitates the communication by becoming an interpreter. Modems translate digital information to analog and analog to digital, acting as an interface between the computer and the phone line.

Like any good interpreter, good modems are fast and accurate. When purchasing a modem be aware of its speed. Modem speed is expressed in bps or bits per second. Early modems transmitted 300 bits per minute. Due to the graphic nature of the Internet, these modems might take from several minutes to several hours to translate the information it takes to display a page of text or graphics. Today, modems are much faster. Most modems translate at 28.8 Kbps or 28,000 bps or faster.

A Telephone Line

A normal telephone line will work fine for connecting to the Internet. While a user is online, the telephone will be busy unless a separate telephone line has been added. Features like call waiting must be turned off during connection time in order not to corrupt the incoming data. Check with the phone company on how to temporarily disable these types of services.

A Service Provider

There are several companies that can provide a connection to the Internet. They are divided into two distinctive groups—Commercial Online Services (COS) and Internet Service Providers (ISP). Commercial Online Services usually provide a range of services within their own network, as well as providing access to the Internet. Internet Service Providers (ISP) provide no services other than e-mail and access to the Internet.

Software

A software package is also necessary to connect and then to view and navigate the Internet. Today almost all of the necessary software is provided in one package. For example, browser software like *Netscape* (Netscape Communications) and *Internet Explorer* (Microsoft) both integrate most all the software you need to use the Internet.

Many ISPs will provide new users with browser software, SLIP (Serial Line Internet Protocol) or PPP (Point to Point Protocol), when they join their service. SLIP and PPP software are the programs that tell a computer to connect with the network.

Commercial Online Services usually will require users to use their software, which is free.

INTERNET TOOLS

ELECTRONIC MAIL

Electronic mail or e-mail is the easiest and most common use of the Internet. An e-mail address allows users to send and receive correspondence with others on the Internet much like you do with regular postal mail. The difference between e-mail and postal mail (commonly called snail mail by online users) is that e-mail is delivered almost immediately. In addition, other electronic materials like documents, files, or programs can be "enclosed" or "attached" to an e-mail message and delivered, along with the message, to the recipient.

When a new user gains Internet access through an Internet Service Provider or a Commercial Network Service, he or she is normally given an e-mail address automatically. These addresses are unique so that computer routers can locate the recipient and deliver the mail. Making mistakes in the spelling, spacing, punctuation, or case may result in the mail being returned undelivered.

The Anatomy of an E-mail Address

E-mail addresses have three distinctive parts as shown in the diagram below:

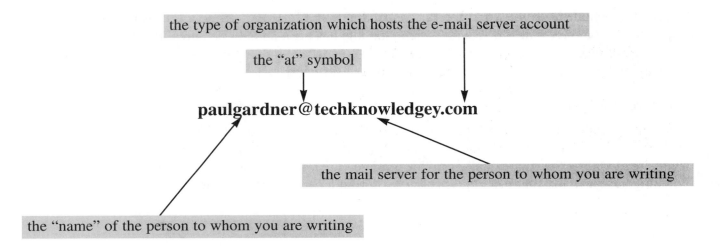

the type of organization which hosts the e-mail server account

the "at" symbol

paulgardner@techknowledgey.com

the mail server for the person to whom you are writing

the "name" of the person to whom you are writing

The suffix after the decimal point indicates what type of service is providing the e-mail account. A few of the suffixes include the following:

Suffix	Type of Provider
.edu	educational
.com	commercial or business
.org	non-profit organization
.gov	government
.mil	military
.net	networking provider

INTERNET TOOLS *(cont.)*

Writing E-mail

Writing a basic e-mail message is simple.

First, launch the e-mail program. This can be done prior to connecting to the Internet or while online. (Refer to your manual for steps to launch your e-mail program.) Most will come up with several directories from which to choose.

In order to send e-mail, choose new mail. This is usually in a menu at the top of the screen or a separate button.

There are two items that are necessary to fill in on the blank e-mail form: the recipient area and the message area. Once the e-mail has been completed, it is either saved for later delivery or sent immediately, depending on whether or not the user is connected.

Other items that can be filled in include the folowing:

- **Subject:** (Optional but recommended) should describe the message
- **CC:** (Optional) e-mail addresses of people to receive a carbon copy of the message
- **BCC:** (Optional) e-mail addresses of people to receive a blind carbon copy (The other recipients will not see the names of BCC recipients in the message.)
- **Reply to:** (Optional) address where a user can receive replies if different from the originator's
- **Date:** (Required and automatic) date and time that the message was sent
- **Expires:** (Optional) date that the message will expire and not be sent

Sending Attachments

Most programs allow users to "attach" or "enclose" electronic files to e-mail. This allows one Internet user to send text files, pictures, sounds, even movies across the Internet. These attached documents can be retrieved or attached by finding the appropriate command or button in the e-mail software being used.

Organizing E-mail

E-mail programs include an address book feature. This feature keeps track of your e-mail addresses by sorting them with the owners' real names. E-mail addresses must be added by the user—it is not done automatically.

E-mail Advice

Most address books allow the user to group e-mail addresses together. This is useful if the user wants to send the same message to many people. For example, a teacher could put all the e-mail addresses of teachers into a group called "Teachers." When that teacher needs materials, ideas, or advice, he or she could send an e-mail request addressed to the whole group. The e-mail is sent to all of the people in the list at the same time.

INTERNET TOOLS *(cont.)*

Receiving E-mail

A commercial Internet service provider has a mail server, a computer that holds mail until a user signs on to retrieve it. To get new mail, the user must first connect to the Internet service. Once connected to the service, the user should start the e-mail software and select the "Get Mail" command.

Note: Some e-mail programs can be configured to automatically retrieve mail when they are started.

The e-mail software will notify the user if there is new mail, though the way each program does it is a little different. Some emit a tone or recorded voice; others simply flash an icon or show an animation. The e-mail will be displayed in a list and organized by date sent, author, and subject.

Replying to and Forwarding E-mail

Once mail has been received, it can be replied to by clicking or choosing Reply. The reply is automatically addressed, and the subject line is filled in with Re: Subject. Most e-mail programs can be set to quote the original note. Quoted lines will be preceded by the > sign.

Forwarding an e-mail to a person is even easier. Clicking or choosing the Forward command will attach the original message to a new e-mail. Just address it to the person to whom the e-mail is being forwarded, add any comments in the message window, and click or choose send.

Emoticons

Although it is customary to make e-mail short and concise, it is not without its whimsical side. It is customary to add to e-mail characters that express emotions. These are normal type characters that look like faces on their sides. A few are listed below.

: - 0	Expresses shock or bewilderment
: -)	Expresses happiness
: - (	Expresses unhappiness
; -)	Indicates an inside joke or sarcasm

What Can Be Done with E-Mail?

Aside from the obvious use of e-mail to communicate with friends and colleagues, e-mail in the classroom can be used for several educational purposes.

- **E-Pals:** Become cyberspace pen pals with other students around the world.

- **Electronic Expeditions:** Students can ask questions and/or read reports on a variety of topics, such as a wagon train going west, the space shuttle, the Iditarod, a South American bike expedition, etc.

- **Request Information:** There are many resources from which parents, students, and teachers can request information for research they are conducting.

- **Collaboration:** Collaborate with other classes or teachers from around the world on projects or lessons.

INTERNET TOOLS *(cont.)*

MAILING LISTS

The advent of e-mail has spawned an exchange of ideas via a tool called mailing lists or listservs. At last estimate there were over 3,000 of these lists, each on a specific topic. To illustrate how this works, let's look at an education example.

A teacher who is interested in sharing ideas with other educators might join a listserv like EDNet. This list boasts over 4,000 members from around the world. Once a member, the teacher could send e-mail messages to the entire group by addressing it to the list. Mailing list members can ask a question, request ideas, or answer the questions of others. Those who join a mailing list become a member of a group of professionals that help each other.

There are two types of listservs: moderated and unmoderated. In a moderated list, an administrator views all the mail and forwards only the good ones to the list members. Many frequently asked questions or FAQs are not forwarded to save list users valuable time. Mail including FAQs is referred to a FAQs file. Other mail which has no value is simply destroyed before it reaches the list members. In comparison, unmoderated lists are as valuable but can waste members' time. Unmoderated lists tend to be self-governing. Members many times will correct other list users' conduct.

Subscribing to a Mailing List

After finding a mailing list to subscribe to, check the list FAQs for the proper procedure on joining. Usually, the following steps are all that are required to join.

1. Create an e-mail message and address it to the mailing list.

2. In the body of the mail, type "subscribe" (without the quotes) <listserv> <Your Name> (e.g., subscribe IECC Pauline Boyd).

3. Some lists prefer just the word "subscribe" to be placed in the subject line. The listserv will use the sender's reply-to e-mail address to automatically forward mail.

Most of the lists are automated, meaning users will be added automatically by the computer that the list resides on. It is important to follow the subscription directions carefully.

Unsubscribing to a Mailing List

Some days it will be impossible to keep up with all of the e-mail being generated by an active list. Going on vacation, working on a project under a deadline, life—all of these things can make it difficult sometimes to interact with the mailing list. It's a good thing that users can unsubscribe as easily as they subscribe. To unsubscribe, what is usually required is to repeat the above directions for subscribing and substitute the word "unsubscribe" in either the subject box or the message box.

An alternative to receiving hundreds of e-mail messages is the digest. Many lists are available in a digest form rather than as separate e-mail messages. This is a convenient format for active lists that generate many messages. Check the mailing list FAQs for availability and instructions for this feature.

INTERNET TOOLS *(cont.)*

SOME EDUCATIONAL MAILING LISTS

BILINGUE-L

Developmental bilingual elementary education list

Address: listserv@Reynolds.k12.or.us.

CHILDRENS-VOICE

Publishes writing from children ages 5-14

Address: listproc@scholnet.carleton.ca.

COSNDISC

Consortium for School Networking

Address: listproc@yukon.cren.org

ECENET-L

Early childhood education list

Address: listserv@uiucvmd.bitnet.

EDINFO-L

Contains information related to educational issues

Address: edinfo-l@iubvm.ucs.indiana.edu

EDTECH

Information on educational technology

Address: listserv@msu.edu

ELEMUG

Elementary School Users' Group

Address: listserv@uicvm.uic.edu.

GRANTS-L

NSF grants information list

Address: listserv@onondaga.bitnet.

IECC

Intercultural E-Mail Classroom Connections

Address: iecc-request@stolaf.edu

K12-AUP

Acceptable Use Policies discussion

Address: k12-aup-request@merit.edu

KIDLINK

Activity projects for kids

Address: listserv@vm1.nodak.edu.

KIDOPEDIA

About creation of the kidopedia sites around the world and related issues

Address:listserv@sjuvm.stjohns.edu

KIDSPHERE

International kid's dialog

Address: kidsphere-request@vms.cis.pitt.edu

MATHSED-L

Discussion group on Mathematics in Education

Address: listserv@deakin.edu.au.

MEDIA-L

Focuses on the role of the media in education

Address: listserv@bingvmb.cc.binghamton.edu

MMEDIA-L

Discussions of multimedia in education

Address: listserv@vmtecmex.bitnet

MIDDLE-L

Discussion of middle school-aged children

Address: listserv@vmd.cso.uiuc.edu.

MUSIC-ED

Music education discussion

Address: listserv@artsedge.kennedy-center.org.

NARST-L

Focuses on teaching science; sponsored by the National Association for Research in Science Teaching

Address: listserv@uwf.bitnet

TAG-L

A Talented and Gifted List

Address: Listserv@ndsuvm1.nodak.edu

UAARTED

Art education discussion

Address: listserv@arizvm1.bitnet.

INTERNET TOOLS *(cont.)*

FILE TRANSFER PROTOCOL

File Transfer Protocol or FTP is what is used to send and receive files. Anything that can be stored on a computer can be sent over the Internet. Documents, pictures, movies, sounds, software programs, etc., can all be sent using FTP. There are millions of shareware and freeware programs that are out there waiting to be downloaded. Choose from millions of lesson plans, digital pictures for reports, video clips for presentations, and books.

Receiving Files

In order to receive or download files using FTP, the following information will be required:

- the URL (address) of the FTP site
- the name of the directory where the file is located
- the name of the file

At one time finding this information was tricky, but since the development of browsers like *Netscape* and *Internet Explorer* and the search engines that are available on the World Wide Web, finding these files is now much easier.

Once you have located the required information for downloading (transferring a file from another computer to yours) a particular file, you will need to use a piece of FTP software to retrieve it. Once again, graphical Internet browser software usually is all you need to carry out the FTP functions that you need to receive files. For this demonstration we will use Netscape Navigator to transfer a shareware program called *GradeKeeper*. Try downloading this file; it is a great grade management program, and you can use it free for 30 days.

1. Log on to your Internet Service Provider or Commercial Online Service. (See Connecting, pages 63.)
2. Once you have connected, start your browser and click the Open button or choose Open from the menu bar.
3. Type in the URL of the site in which the file is located and click Open File.
4. Find the directory in which the file is located and click it to open.
5. Find the file that you wish to download and click it. A copy of the file will download to your computer.

Placing a File

Placing a file or uploading onto another computer is not any more difficult than retrieving; however, most computers are protected from this being done. When retrieving a file from a server (i.e., a computer that is designated to give files) you will normally be using an anonymous FTP site. This means there are no particular security measures for accessing the files. Uploading, on the other hand, is normally done on a secured FTP site. These sites, for obvious reasons, require a password to place files there. If you have an occasion to upload files to a site (as when establishing your own Web page), you will probably be directed as to the procedure needed to do this from the server's administrator. For this reason we will not cover it here.

INTERNET TOOLS *(cont.)*

KEYPALS

As our world becomes more technologically-oriented, e-mail and other forms of electronic information transfer will become an accepted way of communicating. E-mail is already gaining acceptance as a way of transferring information among schools and students. In the world of business, advertising and contact with associates via e-mail is commonplace. For students, even sending messages to their friends or relatives is instructional.

There are a number of curriculum-related activities that you can do with e-mail. For instance, you can get answers to questions about academic subjects, research topics for class reports, or just get another person's (or classroom's) perspective on a particular topic. In addition to learning about our own United States, you can explore and begin to appreciate differences in other societies, cultures, and countries. Personal connections made through e-mail can help you and your students broaden their viewpoints on any number of issues.

E-mail offers a number of potential activities which are relevant to the social studies curriculum. The first thing you as a teacher need to do is to locate "keypals" or "penpals" for your students. Some sources for such projects, as well as classrooms and individuals wishing to correspond with others, are:

> **Epals Classroom Exchange**
> http://www.epals.com/index.html
>
> **E-Mail Key Pal Connection**
> http://www.comenius.com/keypals/index.html
>
> **Intercultural E-Mail Classroom Connection**
> http://www.stolaf.edu/network/iecc/
>
> **Penpal Box**
> http://www.ks-connection.com/penpal/penpal.html/
>
> **Classroom Connect**
> http://www.classroom.net
> This source also lists teachers seeking "keypals" for their students.

INTERNET TOOLS *(cont.)*

Keypal Activity

Using e-mail in a "Keypal" activity is one of the least complicated activities you can use on the Internet. However, a successful student activity depends upon careful and thorough advance planning. Keypal's most common problem is too much unstructured time. To encourage students to stay on task, design a specific evaluation form (see below) to fit your needs.

A keypal activity is appropriate as an instructional strategy if you want to:

- connect students with an expert or mentor on a particular field

- practice a foreign language or learn about another culture or geographic location

- communicate information on relevant topics quickly

- learn how to write the researched information in a clear concise manner.

WEEKLY STUDENT EVALUATION

Project Title_____

Partners' Names_____

Starting Date/Time _____/_____**Completion Date/Time** _____/_____

Keypal name _____ **Total Time Online** _____

Goals_____

Description of Activity_____

_____

_____

Questions That Arose _____

_____

_____

Problems Encountered _____

_____

Solutions to Problems_____

_____

INTERNET TOOLS *(cont.)*

USENET NEWSGROUPS

Usenet groups are much like listservs in that they are dialogs divided into specific subjects. The difference, however, is that Usenet groups are more like a virtual bulletin board. For example, in the teachers' lounge a teacher may place a note asking for lesson plans on that inevitable corkboard that one finds in this oasis of sanity. The teacher returns to the board later in the afternoon and finds ten different lesson plans pinned to the board under the note. This is a simplified explanation of how a Usenet group works. In Usenet, you can read original postings under topical areas of interest and then read responses to those postings. A big difference from listservs is that one does not have to join a Usenet group. One can read any posting under any category.

There are more than 15,000 Usenet message boards (groups), and the number grows every day with subjects ranging from the mundane to the intellectual. The most popular newsgroup categories include the following: computers, business, biology, recreation, science, social issues, miscellaneous, alternative discussions, and, of course, K–12 education. There are more than 400 Usenet groups just devoted to education. Some of these groups are visited by hundreds of people every day while others have few frequenters. It is even possible for one to start his or her own newsgroup.

Most of these groups are unmoderated, meaning anyone can post directly to the group. Moderated newsgroups are censored by a moderator who posts only those messages he or she thinks are of interest to the group. Once the message is posted, anyone can respond.

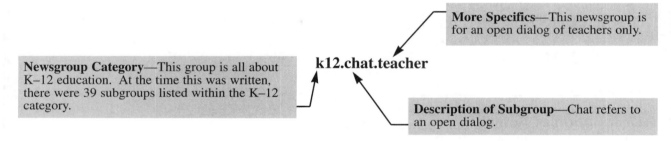

More Specifics—This newsgroup is for an open dialog of teachers only.

k12.chat.teacher

Newsgroup Category—This group is all about K–12 education. At the time this was written, there were 39 subgroups listed within the K–12 category.

Description of Subgroup—Chat refers to an open dialog.

Each newsgroup has a name that is a series of words and abbreviations separated by decimal points or dots, as they have come to be known. A newsgroup name is dissected above.

Subscribing to Newsgroups

"I thought you said that you didn't have to join a newsgroup!" Subscribing is really not a good word, but it is the one that is used. Subscribing to newsgroups is really only choosing the ones that one wants to view and take part in. With over 15,000 newsgroups, there is no way that anyone would want to look at all of them. In fact, some are useless and others downright offensive. So subscribing is just choosing to view certain newsgroups and eliminating the others.

The first thing needed to choose, read, and post newsgroups is a newsreader software program. Today's graphical browsers handle this job well.

INTERNET TOOLS *(cont.)*

1. First, connect to an ISP or COS and launch the newsgroup software.

2. Select View All Newsgroups. This may take a few minutes to complete.

   Note: This may not be ALL the newsgroups that are available. That will depend on your ISP or COS. These companies very seldom provide ALL the newsgroups. If you find out about a newsgroup that is not available through your service, e-mail them and ask that it be added. This can take anywhere from a few minutes to a few hours or days.

3. Next, look at the list and choose the groups that you would like to subscribe to. In *Netscape* it is done by simply clicking a checkmark in the subscribe column. Other software may have you do this differently.

4. Once you have subscribed to all the newsgroups that are of interest to you, select Show Subscribed List to see your newsgroups.

Reading Messages

Reading messages is just a snap. Choose the Newsgroup to view, and a list of those postings will appear.

Click a posting and the message will appear.

Typical Posting

Postings include the following information:

- **Subject:** Make sure that this is short and to the point. If a message is in reference to an original, then it will begin with Re:.

- **Date:** The date and time that the post was made is input automatically.

- **From:** This is the e-mail address of the person who posted the message.

- **Newsgroups:** These are the newsgroups in which the message was posted. Be careful with multiple postings. You should make sure that the message will be appropriate for the newsgroup in which it is posted.

- **Body:** The message itself describes your need or comment as briefly as possible.

Posting Messages

Before posting a message to a Usenet newsgroup, spend a few days reading the existing posts. This is called "lurking." Also read the FAQs (Frequently Asked Questions). These are usually the first postings in a newsgroup. Doing these things will help familiarize one with the protocol for newsgroups and reduce the chance of getting "flamed" (sent a note that is derogatory in nature).

INTERNET TOOLS *(cont.)*

POPULAR EDUCATIONAL USENET NEWSGROUPS

The following is a list of Usenet groups that are popular with K–12 educators.

Learning for the disabled
alt.education.disabled

Children in a split family
alt.child-support

Discussions about raising teenagers
alt.parents-teens

Chat for elementary students
k12.chat.elementary

Chat for middle school students
k12.chat.junior

Chat for teachers
k12.chat.teacher

Art curriculum
k12.ed.art

Teaching computer literacy
k12.ed.comp.literacy

Health and physical education curriculum
k12.ed.health-pe

Home economics and career education
k12.ed.life-skills

Mathematics curriculum
k12.ed.math

Music and performing arts curriculum
k12.ed.music

Science curriculum
k12.ed.science

Social studies and history curriculum
k12.ed.soc-studies

Information for teachers of students with special needs
k12.ed.special

Education for talented and gifted students
k12.ed.tag

Language arts curriculum
k12.lang.art

Bilingual German/English practice with native speakers
k12.lang.deutsch-eng

Bilingual Spanish/English practice with native speakers
k12.lang.esp-eng

THE WORLD WIDE WEB

The World Wide Web, which is also known as WWW or the Web, is the fastest growing segment of the Internet. The reason for the Web's overwhelming success is its ease of navigation and its media-rich environment. Early Internet travelers had to input long strings of text that directed them to their destinations. Once there, they were hampered by having to continually type commands to retrieve information. This is not the case with the WWW.

It is impossible to flip to a page in a magazine or turn to a channel on television these days without receiving an invitation by businesses, government, or educational institutions to visit them on the World Wide Web. Since 1992, this Internet phenomenon has grown somewhere in the neighborhood of 300,000% and although it is now slowing, it continues to grow at an awesome rate. But what is it?

WHAT IS THE WORLD WIDE WEB?

Simply put, the Web is a series of interconnected documents and pages. Using the World Wide Web is like using a super library. One can easily move from site to site, from document to document, from page to film clip, from sound clip to document with millions of different connections to millions of different computers all over the world—thus, a worldwide web of connections.

CONNECTING TO THE WEB

In order to access the Web, one must have a Web browsing program. The most popular browsing programs are *Netscape, Internet Explorer,* and *Mosaic.*

The browsing software will dictate which tools are available. Some browsing programs will allow downloading sounds and digital movies. Web browsers have also integrated older Internet tools like e-mail (electronic mail), FTP (file transfer protocol), TELNET, and other information search tools into one software package. This has made using the Internet simple for even novice users.

Connecting to the World Wide Web is no different than connecting to any other part of the Internet using a browsing program like *Netscape.* Getting to and retrieving information from a Web site is very simple. Just establish a connection with your ISP or COS and launch the browsing program.

WEB PAGES AND WEB SITES

The WWW is based on millions of interconnected electronic pages called Web pages. When one connects to the Web, the first thing that one will see is something called a home page. If a student entered a library looking for information on animals for a report, he or she would first see the sign outside and maybe some directory information to guide him or her to the right part of the library. In Web terms, this would be the home page. A home page is the starting point for an information search. It is the page that the browser automatically goes to when it is started. Most Web browsing programs ship with the publisher's page or the ISP or COS's page as the home page, but this can be changed by the user.

THE WORLD WIDE WEB *(cont.)*

WEB BASICS

Moving around on the Web is very easy. Pointing and clicking a mouse are the only necessary skills, along with a sense of adventure.

Hypertext is context-sensitive text that allows one to move from one page to another simply by clicking on it. Those areas of text that are a different color from the rest are "hyper." Placing the cursor over the colored text causes the arrow to become a hand with a finger pointing. Hypertext links, as they are called, can link to another page and download images, sounds, or even movies..

Hypermedia are pictures that do the same thing as hypertext. Many are in the form of buttons or icons. New Web browsers even allow for animated hypermedia graphics. Most hypermedia graphics are outlined in a color, which is usually blue. However, this is not always the case. Remember, if the cursor turns into a finger when it passes over a graphic, it is probably hyper.

Imagemaps work like hypermedia except clicking different parts of the picture area will take the user to different places. Normally, the picture indicates in some way where the user will be transported when it is clicked.

Automatic (Inline) Graphics are those pictures that load automatically when one arrives at a Web page. Most Web browsers provide the option to view Web pages without these graphics. This will speed up the loading of the page, but it is not very pretty.

Requested Graphics only appear after clicking a link. A blank page appears to display the image. Large pictures can take a long time to download and view. Sometimes Web writers provide users with a thumbnail (i.e., a tiny form of the picture).

NAVIGATING THE WEB

Getting around on the web is not really all that difficult. It is like using the library. If one were looking for information in a library, one would either browse through the aisles looking for the right section (browsing or surfing), go to a librarian and ask for help (directories), or search through a card catalog to locate a specific book or group of books (search engines). The Web offers the same types of options.

BROWSING OR SURFING THE WEB

Every Web page has a uniform resource locator or URL. This is a techie's way of saying address. There are several ways to get to home pages that contain information you want to see. One way is to simply enter the URL of a home page into the Web browser and click the open button. Today, URLs are easy to find. Magazines and television advertise dozens of them. The URL to the White House, one of the most visited home pages on the Web, is

http://www.whitehouse.gov

THE WORLD WIDE WEB *(cont.)*

SEARCH ENGINES

One of the best ways to find information on the Web or any other Internet resource is to use a search engine, the card catalog of the Internet. There are several commercial companies providing search engines free of charge to the public.

To use a search engine, first go to that engine's page. In most cases a form will be presented that allows the input of keywords that the engine will use to search.

UNIFORM RESOURCE LOCATOR

Every resource has a uniform resource locator or URL. Let's look at what these codes mean.

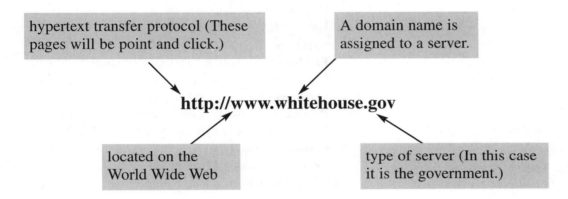

hypertext transfer protocol (These pages will be point and click.)

A domain name is assigned to a server.

http://www.whitehouse.gov

located on the World Wide Web

type of server (In this case it is the government.)

WWW SEARCH ENGINES

The following is a list of good search engines to use when trying to find information on the World Wide Web. Some are education specific, and others have education areas.

Search for WWW, Usenet Newsgroups, and Gopher Sites

Alta Vista http://www.altavista.com/ **Excite** http://www.excite.com/	**HotBot** http://www.hotbot.com/ **Infoseek** http://infoseek.go.com/ **Lycos** http://www.lycos.com/	**Magellan** http://magellan.excite.com/ **Yahoo** http://www.yahoo.com/

Traditional References on the Web

The Electronic Library http://www.elibrary.com **Library Clearinghouse** http://www.clearinghouse.net/ *Shareware* **Shareware.com** http://www.shareware.com	*E-mail Addresses and Personal Home pages* **Yahoo! People Search** http://people.yahoo.com/ **WhoWhere** http://www.whowhere.lycos.com/ **BigFoot** http://www.bigfoot.com/	*Teachers and Kids* **Yahooligans** http://www.yahooligans.com/ **Blue N' Web** http://www.kn.pacbell.com/wired/bluewebn/

THE WORLD WIDE WEB *(cont.)*

WEB CREATION RESOURCES

The following is a list of sites to help you with creating your personal, class, or school Web page:

Web Creation Tools

It used to be that in order to create Web pages, you needed to use a programming language called html. Although it is not difficult to learn, many of us do not want to invest the time. Today many software publishers have created Web authoring tools as easy to use as a WYSIWYG (what you see is what you get) word processor. In fact, many word processors are being marketed now that also author Web pages in this way. The following is a list of just such tools:

Software: *AOLpress*
Producer: America Online, Inc.
URL: http://www.aol.com/

Software: *BBEdit*
Producer: Barebones
URL: http://web.barebones.com/

Software: *FrontPage*
Producer: Microsoft
URL: http://www.microsoft.com/catalog/

Software: *HTMLedInternet*
Producer: Software Technologies
URL: http://www.ist.ca/htmled.html

Software: *HotDog Pro*
Producer: Sausage Software
URL: http://www.sausage.com/

Software: *Home Page*
Producer: Claris Corporation
URL: http://www.claris.com/

Software: *Web Publisher*
Producer: SkiSoft Publishing Corporation
URL: http://www.skisoft.com/

Software: *Netscape Navigator Gold*
Producer: Netscape Communications Corporation
URL: http://home.netscape.com/index.html

Software: *PageMill*
Producer: Adobe Corporation
URL: http://www.adobe.com/prodindex/main.html

Web Creation Tutors

There are several places on the Web to find out how to author for the Web. Here are a few:

Web66

> http://www.ncsa.uiuc.edu/General/Internet/WWW/HTMLPrimer.html

World Wide Web Workbook

> http://www.fi.edu/primer/setup.html

Tutorials

> http://www.geocities.com/Athens/8281/

Weave Your Web

> http://www.msg.net/tutorial/

Page Templates and Free Graphics

One doesn't have to be an expert at design and layout to utilize all those neat little buttons, bullets, icons, lines, and animated goodies that are on Web pages. They can be downloaded, almost always for free, and used immediately. An excellent resource for finding these freebies is at **Yahoo's Directory**:

> http://dir.yahoo.com/Computers_and_Internet/

INTEGRATING THE INTERNET INTO LESSON PLANS

There is so much information on the Internet, making the connection with this technology is more of a joy than a chore. The Internet can make a job more efficient and creative. However, using technology tools can be awkward and slow at first. Do not give up. As the in's and out's of the Internet become more familiar, this electronic playground of information can make your teaching more pleasurable.

1. Find an Internet site that is related to the curriculum. This can be easily done by using one of the many search engines available on the Web.

2. Think about the lessons that are taught within the units of study. Search through the sites to find appropriate sites that enhance the lessons. There are several kinds of sites that can benefit teaching and learning in different ways. Some are listed below:

   Internet Research: Those sites that are not necessarily written for K–12 education might have media and/or research that can be used in students' projects or as visual aids in lessons.

   Internet Projects: These sites are dedicated to providing students with activities in which to collaborate with other students all over the world.

   Virtual Field Trips: Students take part in the adventures in which students communicate with experts in the field.

   Publishing on the Internet: These sites publish student projects for the whole world to see.

   Internet Related and Non-Internet Related Lesson Plans: Several organizations publish lesson plans on the Internet. A lot of these integrate curriculum with technology tools; others are simply good non-technology related lesson plans.

3. Implement the lessons at an appropriate comfort level. It might be best to use the Internet as a personal resource at first. Gathering media and lesson plans is not difficult, but virtual field trips, publishing, and projects require much more effort. After becoming comfortable with the Internet, these more interactive activities will be very enjoyable and educational.

The most important thing to remember is that this new media is nothing but a tool. How the tool is used will determine the level of success.

WELCOME TO YOUR NEW SCHOOL

Wouldn't it be wonderful to start the school year and have a resource that introduced you to the faculty, staff, and facilities of your new school? This project will help your students get to know their new school and introduce them to the computer programs and peripherals available to them.

The finished product will be a *HyperStudio* presentation that may be used to introduce new students and families to the school.

Grade level: six

Duration: 30 to 40 minutes on the computer

Materials: *HyperStudio* planning sheets, Welcome to Your New School planning sheet, digital camera (optional), scanner (optional)

Procedure

Before the Computer

To complete this project, students will be responsible for interviewing faculty and stafff members. They will also need to visit the different areas of the school. Be sure to warn students about any "off limits" areas.

- Develop a list of personnel to be interviewed, including the principal, assistant principal, teachers, para-professionals, and support personnel.

- Create a list of areas of the school such as media center, cafeteria, gym, computer lab, library, etc.

- Provide your students with guidelines for gathering their information.

- Use the Welcome to your New School planning sheet to make sure all students gather the same kind of information.

- Work together with your students to formulate questions that interest them.

- If available, use the digital camera to take pictures of activities and the scanner to scan and save pictures out of annuals, etc.

On the Computer

Select a student who knows *HyperStudio* or a similar program to be in charge of creating the introductions. If using your classroom computer, allow each student to create a card, importing graphics and text fields. Always save after each card.

A *HyperStudio* planning sheet has been filled out as an example on page 83. A blank, reproducible form appears in the Resources and Additional References section of this book.

WELCOME TO YOUR NEW SCHOOL

PLANNING SHEET

Name of Person: _____

Job at School: _____

Education: _____

Interest/Hobbies: _____

Special Interest Questions:

1.   How did you get involved in education?

_____

_____

2.

_____

_____

3.

_____

_____

4.

_____

_____

_____

_____

WELCOME TO YOUR NEW SCHOOL

PLANNING SHEET *(cont.)*

Building Visited: _____

Building's Function: _____

1. Briefly describe the building you visited. Be sure to include details such as colors, the location of the entrances and exits, and its location on the school grounds.

_____

_____

_____

_____

_____

_____

_____

_____

_____

_____

2. On a separate piece of paper, draw a map of your school. Be sure to include where your classes are and mark the building you described above with an **X**.

HYPERSTUDIO PLANNING SHEET

Title Card

Buttons/Links: __Use point finger icon with the title.__
WELCOME TO FILMORE MIDDLE SCHOOL
__(Include picture of school if available.)__

Notes (Text/Sounds/Animations):
Next-dissolve transition
Use font size 24.

Card 1

Buttons/Links: __Make button invisible.__
This is our Principal, Mr. Smith
__(Include picture of principal if available.)__

Notes (Text/Sounds/Animations):
Next-dissolve transition
Use font size 10; make background light blue.
Picture links to next card

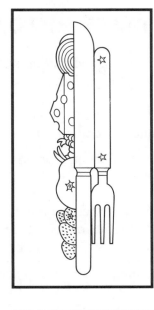

Card 2

Buttons/Links: __Make button invisible.__
Our secretary greets guests as they come to visit.
__(Include picture of secretary if available.)__

Notes (Text/Sounds/Animations):
Next-dissolve transition
Use font size 10; make background light green.
Picture links to next card

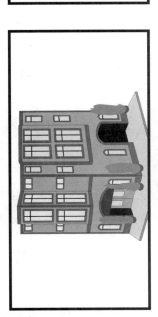

Card 3

Buttons/Links: __Make button invisible.__
Let's visit the media center.
__(Include picture of media lab if available.)__

Notes (Text/Sounds/Animations):
Next-dissolve transition
Use font size 10; make background light yellow.
picture links to next card

Card 4

Buttons/Links: __Make button invisible.__
This is Mr. Jones, our Media Specialist
__(Include picture of Mr. Jones if available.)__

Notes (Text/Sounds/Animations):
Next-dissolve transition
Use font size 10; make background light blue.
Picture links to next card

Card 5

Buttons/Links: __Make button invisible.__
Hungry? let's visit the cafeteria!
__(Include picture of cafeteria with students eating.)__

Notes (Text/Sounds/Animations):
Next-dissolve transition
Use font size 10; make background red. Picture
links to next card

BLACK HISTORY MONTH PROJECT

Students will learn organization and editing skills while researching famous black people in preparation for Black History Month. This project can be used as a template for simliar projects in other subjects.

Grade level: six to eight

Duration: 35 to 45 minutes on computer

Materials: Biographical Data Sheet, *HyperStudio* planning sheets

Procedure:

Students will use *HyperStudio* to create a presentation of 8 to 10 cards to introduce their subject, including a title frame and credit frame. Students will use planning sheets to organize their presentation. If you have access to the lab, begin with a mini-lesson to create the title page.

This project is a good candidate for a group activity, with students dividing the tasks of research and stack development.

Before the Computer:

- Students will use an electronic encyclopedia or whatever resources are available to research their subject.

- Students will record subject's biographical information and important contributions on handout.

- Students will use planning sheet to organize presentation, write captions, and determine graphics to be used.

On the Computer:

- Students should use *HyperStudio* to create cards with collected information.

- Title card should have the subjects name and the student's name.

- Card 1 should have place and date of birth.

- Card 2 should have place and date of death.

- Card 3 should have an early-life adventure.

- Card 4 should include the subject's educational background.

- Card 5 should have marriage/family information.

- Card 6 should have major contributions/accomplishments.

- Cards 7–10 will list other information.

- Students will select border and background colors and set other options such as buttons.

- When all projects are completed, students will present them to the class.

A Biographical Data Sheet has been filled out as an example on page 85. A blank, reproducible form appears in the Resources and Additional References section of this book.

BIOGRAPHICAL DATA SHEET

Student Name: <u>Maria Vasquez</u>   Due <u>12/01/99</u>

Research Topic <u>Louis Armstrong</u>

INFORMATION TO RESEARCH AND RECORD

Date of birth: <u>1901</u>

Date of death (if applicable):   <u>1971</u>

Place of birth: <u>New Orleans</u>

Early life: <u>As a teenager, he played in jazz bands in the New Orleans area.</u>

Education: <u>There was no information about his education in the reference materials.</u>

Marriage/Family: <u>There was no information about his family life in the reference materials.</u>

Major contributions/accomplishments: <u>Louis Armstrong made a series of popular records such as</u>

<u>"Potato Head Blues," "West End Blues," and "Cornet Chop Suey." He also appeared in the movies</u>

<u>*High Society* and *Hello Dolly*.</u>

Other information: _____

FAMOUS BLACK AMERICANS

Louis Armstrong	Benjamin Hooks
Crispus Attucks	Langston Hughes
Benjamin Banneker	Jesse Jackson
Mary McLeod Bethune	Scott Joplin
Ralph Bunche	Barbara Jordan
George W. Carver	Martin Luther King, Jr.
Shirley Chisholm	Malcolm X
Frederick Douglass	Thurgood Marshall
Charles Drew	Rosa Parks
W. E. B. DuBois	Adam Clayton Powell, Jr.
Paul Dunbar	Sojourner Truth
Duke Ellington	Harriet Tubman
Dizzy Gillespie	Nat Turner
Nikki Giovanni	Booker T. Washington
John Henry	Phillis Wheatley
Billie Holiday	Andrew Young

REVIEW THE PARTS OF SPEECH

Is it a noun or a verb? This activity will allow students to review the parts of speech studied in the classroom while using special keys and discovering options in a word processing program.

Grade level: six to eight

Duration: 20 to 30 minutes computer time

Materials: *ClarisWorks* or other word processing program, student writing

Procedure:

Before the Computer:

- Review all the parts of speech to be covered in this activity or use it for review to check on the students' understanding.

- Students should use some writing they have already finished. It would be a good idea for students to label the the parts of speech on the copy of the writing they will be entering into the computer.

On the Computer:

- Students will type in their paragraph.

- The text style of each part of speech will be changed to correspond with the directions.

- Use the following:

      Nouns—Bold

      Verbs—Italic

      Adjectives—Shadow

      Adverbs—Underline

      Prepositions—Double underline

Tip:

You may want to use a story written by the entire class. This way they will already be familiar with the text to be modified.

YOU ARE THE EDITOR

Students will use organization, writing, and editing skills while designing and publishing the front page of a newsletter. This project can be adapted for any subject.

Grade level: six to eight

Duration: 35 to 45 minutes on computer

Materials: *Writing Center* Planning Worksheet

Procedure:

Students will use the *Writing Center* and information from a book of their choice or a teacher-assigned book to design the front page of a newsletter. Students will select appropriate graphics for their newsletter.

Before the Computer:

- Students will read a book. Characters and settings from the book will be used to generate information for their newsletter.
- Students should have a working knowledge of the *Writing Center* or other publishing software. (See Software Shortcuts: *The Writing Center*)
- Using the newsletter planning worksheet, students will design the front page with some of the following sections:

  editorial

  advertisement

  upcoming events

  birth and/or death announcements

  wedding announcements

  other sections or information students would like to include

On the Computer:

- Using the *Writing Center*, students will choose Newsletter from the choice menu.
- Students will select font, size, and graphics to use with the text for their newsletter front page.
- Students will save on disk and print a copy for display and assessment.

A *Writing Center* Planning Worksheet has been filled out as an example on page 89. A blank, reproducible form appears in the Resources and Additional References section of this book.

WRITING CENTER PLANNING WORKSHEET *(cont.)*

Student: _____William Peterson_____   Book Title: _____The Hobbit_____

Illustration

Illustration

Text: _____Upcoming Events: Bilbo Baggins, formerly of the Shire, will soon be holding an estate sale to liquidate his assets. The sale is being handled by his closest cousin. "I knew he would come to no good end!"_____

Text: _____Obituary: Finally laid to rest today, Smaug, that old scourge of the dwarf kingdom and Lake Town. It is rumored that an arrow shot by Bard of Lake Town was the one that brought an end to Smaug's reign of terror. "Hey, I was just doing my job," the modest archer was overheard to say during the following celebrations._____

USING THE THESAURUS

Student word choice can be improved using a thesaurus. This project will help your students become better acquainted with the benefits and use of a thesaurus.

Grade level: six to eight

Duration: 20 to 30 minutes on computer

Materials: *ClarisWorks* or other word processing program with a thesaurus, example of student writing

Procedure:

Before the Computer

- Have students write several descriptive paragraphs.
- Explain what a thesaurus is—a list of synonyms that will help them find words with the same meanings.
- Go over some examples of synonyms.
- Tell students where to find and how to use the thesaurus on the word processing program.

Examples:

It poured so hard that we had to run into the empty shelter.
        poured = rained, drizzled, showered
        empty = vacant, bare, clear

Remind students when using a thesaurus to choose a word which is the same part of speech. Students should also be aware of the connotative differences in words, even though they may be similar in meaning. A sentence can easily say something very different if the word substituted for another carries more emotional or connotative weight.

On the Computer:

- Have students type in their paragraph in the word processing module. Students need to edit their paragraph for spelling (use the spelling checker), punctuation, and structure.
- Students should next copy their paragraph and paste a second copy below the first.
- In the second paragraph, students can select a word by highlighting it, go to Edit in the menu bar, Writing Tools, and choose Thesaurus. Highlight the word to replace the word in the text and click on Replace.
- The students should repeat the above step until the required number of changes has been made.
- After proofing their paragraph, students will print a hard copy to be turned in to the teacher.

CLASSROOM JOURNAL/NEWSLETTER

This class project will result in a newsletter to be printed and sent home at the end of each month or grading period, whichever the class decides. It is important to keep parents informed, and this is the ideal way in which to keep parents aware of what you are doing.

Grade level: six to eight

Duration: approximately 5 minutes at the end of each class period on computer

Materials: *ClarisWorks* or other word processing program

Procedure:

A template (or stationery) should be designed and saved for the newsletter ahead of time. Working alphabetically, at the end of each class period or the next day, a student will type in news from the day, including special events or happenings. At the end of the month, chosen students will edit and print the newsletter for all students to take home to their parents. If teachers are team teaching, you may want to include events from all classes and send the newsletter home as a team newsletter. The template could include an icon or graphic for the class.

Before the Computer:

- Before beginning, explain the procedure to the students. You may want to discuss some of the activities that might be included in the newsletter.
- A list of students can be placed near the computer so they will know when it is their turn to record events on the computer.

On the Computer:

- At the end of the class period or if it is decided to include other class events, at the end of the next days class period, the assigned students will enter class activities on the template including his or her name as the reporter for that day.
- At the end of the designated time period, assigned students will edit the script, adding graphics if applicable. Assigned students will run a copy of the newsletter for all students.

Tip:

To assure success for all students, each month assign a student to be the assistant should a student need help. This student would also make sure that the assigned student typed in the daily activities, double-checked for spelling, and printed the final copy.

WHAT'S YOUR GENRE

Do your students know what you mean when discussing the genre of a book? Let's make a list.

Grade level: six to eight

Duration: 20 minutes on the computer

Materials: *The Writing Center*, book from a genre currently being studied, planning sheet

Procedure

Before the Computer:

- After a class discussion of the different genres, students will choose or be assigned a book from a genre in their reading.
- Students will read the book and record information on the information sheet. They will need to correct errors, check for complete sentences, etc., so computer time will go quickly.

On the Computer:

- Using *The Writing Center*, students will choose Report or Letter from the menu.
- Students will set the margins, font, and style of text.
- Next the students will select a heading.
- The heading of their report should be the title of the book in large letters and the author's under the title in smaller print. A picture should be placed with the heading.
- Students should proofread their story, save to their disk, and print a hard copy.

Extended Activity:

Students could read the story in front of the class to reinforce the genre and practice public speaking skills. Extra credit could be given for the use of props or animation.

TAKE THE QUIZ

Help your students learn how to use *HyperStudio* to enhance problem-solving skills in math. Students can work as a team or individually to create a math quiz using a *HyperStudio* stack.

Grade level: six to eight

Duration: 30 to 40 minutes on the computer

Materials: *HyperStudio* planning sheets

Procedure:

This project can be designed to be used with any math unit you are studying. Students will make up math problems to correlate with the unit and design a *HyperStudio* project of as many cards as you feel they will have time to enter.

Before the Computer:

- Students will work in teams or individually, depending on your circumstances.

- On planning sheets, in addition to a title card, students will make up 5 cards with problems for others to solve. They will link with buttons indicating correct or incorrect answers and illustrating how they arrived at the correct answer.

- These problems can be taken from the unit you are studying. It should give some indication as to the understanding of the students.

On the Computer:

- On the first card of the stack, students will introduce the math concept, for example, "Factoring Large Numbers." The card will have a button linking the first card to the next card.

- On the second card, students will add a text box with a problem and four possible answers.

- Students will place buttons beside each answer.

- A negative sound will be added to the buttons with the wrong answer and also a link to a card which illustrates how to arrive at the answer but does not reveal the answer.

- The correct answer will have a positve sound and link to the next problem.

- Continue this process until the project is complete.

MEASURE YOUR SMILE

Metric measurement is often confusing to students who are used to the English system of weights and measures. In this activity students will use a metric ruler to measure smiles and learn how to use a spreadsheet to create a graph of the results.

Grade level: six to eight

Duration: 20 to 30 minutes on computer

Materials: *ClarisWorks* or any spreadsheet program with graphing and metric capability

Before the Computer:

- Divide students into even groups.

- Have one student act as the recorder for each group.

- Each student in the group will use the metric ruler to measure the length of the smile of every member of his or her group.

- The recorder lists the person's name and the length of the his or her smile in centimeters.

- After comparing results, the smiles can be measured again for verification, or students may proceed to the computer component.

On the Computer:

- Open the spreadsheet module from *ClarisWorks*.

- Label Column A **Names**. Type in the names of each student in this column.

- Label Column B **Length**. Type in the length of each smile in this column.

- Highlight the data in the two columns and select **Make Chart** from the Options menu.

- Choose **Bar Graph.**

- Label the X and Y axes.

- Print the bar graph.

- Now go back to **Make Chart** and choose **Pie Graph**.

- Uncheck the color option unless you have a color printer.

- Title the graph.

- In Series, check **Label Data** and then check **% to be displayed**.

- Print the pie graph.

Have the students compare their bar graph with their pie graph. Which graph better represents and displays their data?

MEASURE YOUR SMILE *(cont.)*

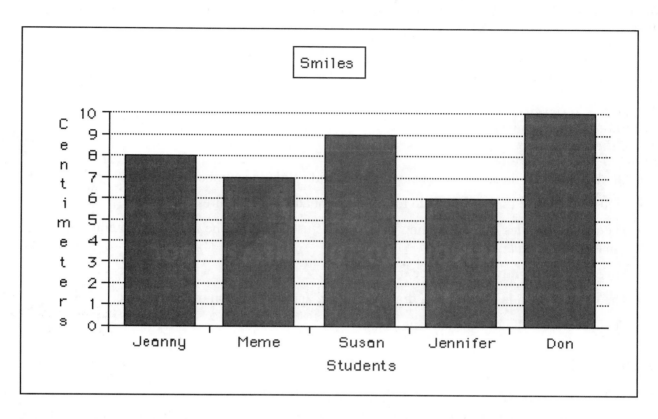

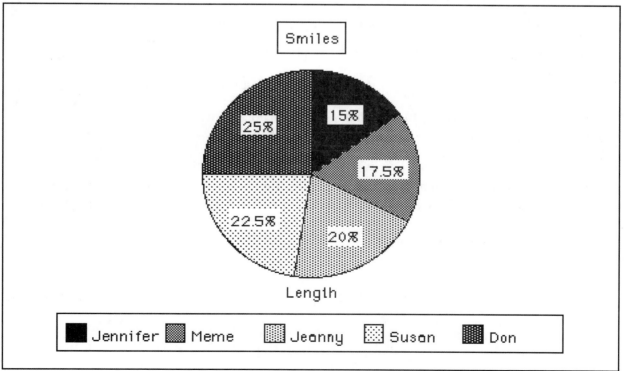

GEOMETRIC FIGURES

There are many different kinds of geometric figures that have names. Students need to become familiar with the names of these figures as well as their definitions.

Grade level: six to eight

Duration: 30 to 40 minutes on computer

Materials: *ClarisWorks* planning sheet

Before the Computer:

- On the planning sheet the students will have a title slide for number one.
- Students will use the second slide to introduce quadrilateral figures.
- The next five slides of the planning sheet will be used to draw the five quadrilateral figures, giving names and explanations.
- Slide number eight will introduce triangles.
- The next three slides will have a drawing, name, and explanation of the triangle.
- The last slide will have the student's name.

On the Computer:

- Students will choose Word Processing from the choices given.
- Students will use *ClarisWorks* to type in and draw pictures, following their planning sheet.
- Students will choose slide show and choose options of background color, etc.
- Students will save their slide show to present to the class.

Tip:

Under View in the menu bar, have student click on Show Tools. This will help students as they are drawing their figures. Students should limit the amount of text to two or three sentences to describe the geometric figure.

A *ClarisWorks* slide show planning sheet has been filled out as an example on page 97. A blank, reproducible form appears in the Resources and Additional References section of this book.

GEOMETRIC FIGURES *(cont.)*

Storyboard Planning Sheet

Name: <u>Melissa Horowitz</u>   Project: <u>Geometric Shapes</u>

**MY
GEOMETRY
SLIDES**

Slide # <u>One</u>

Words/Narration: <u>My Geometry Slides</u>

**QUADRILATERAL
FIGURES**

Slide # <u>Two</u>

Words/Narration: <u>Quadrilateral Figures</u>

<u>A quadrilateral figure is any figure that consists</u>

<u>of four sides. There are five kinds of quadri-</u>

<u>lateral figures: square, rectangle, rhombus,</u>

<u>trapezoid, and parallelogram.</u>

THE SQUARE

THE FOUR SIDES OF THE SQUARE
ARE OF EQUAL LENGTH.
EACH OF THE FOUR ANGLES
OF THE SQUARE IS NINETY
DEGREES. THE OPPOSING SIDES
OF A SQUARE ARE PARALLEL.

Slide # <u>Three</u>

Words/Narration: <u>The Square</u>

<u>The four sides of the square are of equal length.</u>

<u>Each of the four angles of the square is ninety</u>

<u>degrees. The opposing sides of a square are</u>

<u>parallel.</u>

THE RECTANGLE

THE RECTANGLE HAS OPPOSING
SIDES OF EQUAL LENGTH.
OPPOSITES SIDES ARE PARALLEL.
THE ANGLES ARE ALL
NINETY DEGREE ANGLES.

Slide # <u>Four</u>

Words/Narration: <u>The Rectangle</u>

<u>The rectangle has opposing sides of equal length.</u>

<u>Opposite sides are parallel. The angles are all</u>

<u>ninety degree angles.</u>

LONG DIVISION SLIDE SHOW

Long division can be difficult for students to understand when the quotient has two or more numbers and the dividend has three or more numbers with remainders. This project will allow the student to go through the process and will better understand that process.

Grade level: six

Duration: 30 minutes on computer

Materials: *ClarisWorks* slide show planning sheet

Before the Computer:

- During the unit on long division, have the students each choose a long division problem. One problem will result in five or more slides.

- Each student should solve the problem on a piece of blank paper. Have the student break the problem down into steps. You may want to give an example for the students so they will understand the steps in breaking down the problem.

- Use the *ClarisWorks* planning sheet to illustrate each step in the process of their long division problem.

- Each slide should include an explanation of the process. This is very important if you are to know if the student really understands the process.

On the Computer:

- Use the *ClarisWorks* word processing program to type in all information.

- Each step of the process should be on a different page.

- Go to Format and Insert Page Break at the end of each step.

Example:

Page 1: Show the problem.

Page 2: Solve the first part of the problem with an explanation of that process.

Page 3: Continue to the next step in solving the problem with the explanation of that process.

UNDERSTANDING METRIC CONVERSION

What student doesn't enjoy sitting down to their favorite food and digging in?. In this project, students will have the opportunity to share their favorite recipe and convert the measurements form the English system to the metric system. The collected set of recipes should be included in a class cookbook.

Grade level: six to eight

Duration: 20 to 30 minutes on computer

Materials: *ClarisWorks* or any word processing program, planning sheet

Procedure:

Before the Computer:

- Share cooking measurements and tools with the students. Most cooking tools give both metric and customary units.
- Discuss the abbreviations used for cooking measurements opposed to measuring other objects such as football fields, etc.
- Have students bring in a favorite recipe.
- Talk about the measurements in their recipe and how to convert.
- Discuss the problems that might occur if you were to convert a measurement in the wrong amounts.
- Set up a template on the computer so the students can type in their recipe with measurements and directions for cooking. Remind students they should Save As not Save when they have finished typing their recipe. (If they Save, it will save over the template.)

On the Computer:

- Allow students to type in their recipes, selecting graphics for their page or use the paint program to draw their graphics.
- Several students can use the paint program to design dividers to separate the different categories of foods.
- Consider allowing your students to bring in prepared versions of their recipes. A metric conversion table has been included for you to reproduce.

RECIPE FOR SUCCESS!

Student Name: _____   Date: _____

Name of Recipe: _____

Category: (ex., breads, main dish) _____

Preheat oven to _____   Serves _____

Ingredients

Metric   English

_____   _____

_____   _____

_____   _____

_____   _____

_____   _____

_____   _____

_____   _____

Directions

_____

_____

_____

_____

_____

_____

_____

METRIC CONVERSIONS

Linear

100 cm	=	1 meter
cm	=	centimeter
1/4"	=	.6 cm
1/2"	=	1.3 cm
1"	=	2.54 cm
3"	=	7.62 cm
6"	=	15.24 cm
9"	=	22.86 cm
12"	=	30.48 cm
18"	=	45.72 cm
24"	=	61 cm
36"	=	91.44 cm
100 yds	=	91.4 m
1 mile	=	1,609 m

Volume (dry and liquid)

L	=	liter
mL	=	milliliter = .001 L
1 tsp	=	5 mL
1 T	=	15 mL
1/4 c	=	59 mL
1/2 c	=	118 mL
1 c	=	236 mL
8 oz	=	.236 L
1 oz	=	30 mL
1 pt	=	about .5 L (473.2 mL)
1 qt	=	about 1 L (946.4 mL)
1 gal	=	about 3.8 L
1 L	=	1.0567 qts liquid
1 qt dry	=	1.101 L
1 qt liquid	=	.09463 L
1 gal liquid	=	3.78541 L

Temperatures

To convert Fahrenheit to Celsius
(F° - 32 x .55)

To convert Celsius to Fahrenheit
(C° x 1.8) + 32

	C	F
boiling point of water	100°	212°
freezing point of water	0°	32°
cold day	-20°	-4°
room temperature	20°	66°
body temperature	37°	98.6°

Oven Temperatures

	C	F
warm oven	135°	275°
moderate oven	175°	350°
hot oven	204°	400°

Weights

1 gram	=	0.03527 ounce
1 ounce	=	28.35 grams
1 kilogram	=	2.2046 lbs
1 pound	=	453.4 grams
	or	454 kilograms
1 ton	=	908 kilograms

WOMEN IN MATH AND SCIENCE

Many women have influenced the direction of math and science. This project will introduce students to women who made a difference.

Grade level: six to eight

Duration: 30 minutes on the computer

Materials: *ClarisWorks* word processing, Biographical Data Sheet

Before the Computer:

- Students will be assigned a person to research.
- Students will use the electronic encyclopedia or other resources to research and record information on the planning sheet.
- Students will find a picture of their subject either to be scanned or saved as a graphic from an electronic encyclopedia or the Internet.
- A one-page rough draft will be written from the notes taken.

On the Computer:

- Students will use choose the word processing module in *ClarisWorks*.
- For the heading of their report, students will select the Times font, 24-point size, and bold text style.
- If students found pictures, place the pictures in the heading.
- Use the 4-point line tool to place a line under the title.
- The body of the report will be justified, Times font, 12-point size, and plain text style with indentions at the beginning of each paragraph.
- A one-page report will be typed.
- Edit the paragraph for spelling (use the spelling checker), punctuation, and structure.
- Print a hard copy and also save to a disk.

A Biographical Data Sheet has been filled out as an example. A blank, reproducible form appears in the Resources and Additional References section of this book.

WOMEN IN MATH AND SCIENCE *(cont.)*

Ada Byron-Lovelace
First Computer Programmer

Barbara McClintock
Cytologist

Caroline Lucretia Herschel
Mathematician, Astronomer

Dian Fossey
American Naturalist, Primatologist, Zoologist

Elizabeth Blackwell
First Woman Doctor

Elizabeth Garrett Anderson
First British Woman Doctor

Emilie du Chatelet
Mathematician

Emmy Noether
Algebraist

Evelyn Boyd Granville
Aftrican American Mathematician & Astronomer

Florence Nightingale
Nurse, Statistician, Reformer

Grace Murray Hopper
Computer Pioneer, Admiral

Hypathia
Mathematician

Jane Goodall
Primatologist, Zoologist

Judith Love Cohen
Apollo System Engineer (NASA)

Julia Bowman Robinson
Mathematician, Statistician

Maria Gaetana Agnesi
Mathematician

Maria Mitchell
Early American Astronomer

Marie Sklodowska Curie
Chemist/Physicist, Winner of 2 Nobel Prizes

Mary Ellen Estill Rudin
Mathematician

Mary Fairfax Somerville
Mathematician

Mary Gray
Mathematician

Rachel Carson
Environmentalist/Author

Rosalyn Sussman Yalow
Physicist, Research Scientist

Sophie German
Mathematician

INTERNET ECOLOGISTS

Students and teachers will enjoy participating in the Internet project. GLOBE (Global Learning and Observations to Benefit the Environment) is a public-private partnership sponsored by the National Oceanic and Atmospheric Administration, the National Aeronautics and Space Administration, the National Science Foundation, the Environmental Protection Agency, and others.

Grade: six to eight

Duration: one hour each week during the school year on the computer

Materials: Internet access

Procedure:

Go to http://www.globe.gov to register your class for this project.

Before the Computer:

- Look in an atlas to find locations of other schools from across the globe participating in the project.
- Explain the project objectives which you get off the Internet to the students so they will know the scope of the project.
- Create several "hotspots" for observation. If you are near a river or lake, stake off a 10-kilometer area and about a 30 by 30 meters space on the school's grounds to be used for observations and data collection.

On the Computer:

- Bookmark the GLOBE site http://www.globe.gov.
- Visit the site with your students. If possible, do so with with a large-screen television.
- When the project gets underway, your class can begin sending their environmental measurements to GLOBE headquarters.

TRACK YOUR STATE'S WEATHER

Students will use process and manipulative skills as they discover weather concepts about a state. This will be an exciting exercise illustrating the potential for communication and research using the Internet.

Grade level: six to eight

Duration: 20 to 30 minutes on the computer

Materials: computer with Internet access, activity sheet

Before the Computer:

- The class will discuss weather forecasting terms, vocabulary, and concepts of movement.
- Students will choose or be assigned a state to research.
- Students will need to use an electronic encyclopedia or other source to choose four major cities in that state. (**Hint:** Students may want to have five just in case the cities they choose are not listed at the Internet site.)
- Discuss how you can determine if a city can be considered major. (ex. capital, population, dot on map or color/shade of print)

On the Computer:

- Using the search engine Web Crawler, type in "The Weather Channel Home page" and bookmark this site.
- Students will go to The Weather Channel and click on Weather Current Conditions.
- Next go to Current Conditions and Five-Day Forecasts for over 1,200 cities.
- Click on the first letter of the state chosen or click on the state on the map.
- Locate four cities listed for your state and write the information on the activity sheet for each city.

Options:

Students may want to share their findings. Let them create a bulletin board displaying their research.

TRACK YOUR STATE'S WEATHER

Name _____   State _____

Date and day of the week: _____

First City _____

What are today's weather conditions for the city?

_____

_____

Second City_____

What are today's weather conditions for the city?

_____

_____

Third City _____

What are today's weather conditions for the city?

_____

_____

Fourth City _____

What are today's weather conditions for the city?

_____

_____

GRAPH YOUR STATE'S WEATHER

Students will use the same process and manipulative skills as they record weather conditions in four cities of a different state and make a graph.

Grade level: six to eight

Duration: 20 to 30 minutes on the computer

Materials: computer with Internet access, activity sheet, *ClarisWorks* or any spreadsheet program with graphing capability

Before the Computer:

- Using the search engine Web Crawler, type in "The Weather Channel Home page" and bookmark this site.

- The class will review weather forecasting, terms, vocabulary, and concepts of movement.

- Students will choose or be assigned a different state to research.

- Students will need to use electronic encyclopedia or other source to choose four major cities in that state. (Students may want to have five just in case the cities they choose are not listed at the Internet site.)

- Discuss how you can determine if a city can be considered major. (ex., capital, population, dot on map or color/shade of print)

On the Computer:

- Students will go to The Weather Channel and click on Weather Current Conditions.

- Next go to Current Conditions and Five-Day Forecasts for over 1,200 cities.

- Click on the first letter of the state chosen or click on the state on the map.

- Locate four cities listed for the state and write the information on the activity sheet for each city.

- Use the *ClarisWorks* spreadsheet module to create at least two different graphs for reporting the data. (See the lesson plan for Measure Your Smile for more information on using the graphing capabilities of *ClarisWorks*.)

For this activity, students can discuss the various graphs and which one is designed to best display their data.

GRAPH YOUR STATE'S WEATHER *(cont.)*

Student's name _____ State _____

First City _____

Date: _____ High Temperature: _____

Date: _____ High Temperature: _____

Date: _____ High Temperature: _____

Second City_____

Date: _____ High Temperature: _____

Date: _____ High Temperature: _____

Date: _____ High Temperature: _____

Third City _____

Date: _____ High Temperature: _____

Date: _____ High Temperature: _____

Date: _____ High Temperature: _____

Fourth City _____

Date: _____ High Temperature: _____

Date: _____ High Temperature: _____

Date: _____ High Temperature: _____

SCIENTIST RESEARCH PROJECT

Students will use organization and editing skills while researching famous scientists and then present a slid show based on their final document.

Grade level: six to eight

Duration: 35 to 45 minutes on computer

Materials: *ClarisWorks*, research sheet, *ClarisWorks* slide show planning sheets

Procedure:

This activity introduces students to setting up and editing computer-generated documents. Students will use the *ClarisWorks* slide show to create a presentation of 8 slides to introduce their subject, including a title frame and credit frame.

Before the Computer:

- Students will use an electronic encyclopedia to research their subject.
- Students will record their subject's biographical information and important contributions on the handout.
- Students will use a planning sheet to organize their presentation, write captions, and determine graphics to be used.

On the Computer:

- Students will select the word processing module from *ClarisWorks*.
- Students should input their information and import graphics, remembering to save often.
- After checking for spelling, students will choose Slide Show under View from the menu.
- Students will select border and background colors and set other options.

When all projects are completed, students will present their slide show to the class.

A *ClarisWorks* slide show planning sheet has been filled out as an example. A blank, reproducible form appears in the Resources and Additional References section of this book.

FAMOUS SCIENTISTS

Archimedes	Edward Jenner
Aristotle	Johannes Kepler
Robert Boyle	Robert Koch
Auguste Comte	Arthur Kornberg
Nicolaus Copernicus	Charles Lyell
John Dalton	James Clerk Maxwell
Charles Darwin	Gregor Mendel
Euclid	Dmitri Mendeleev
Michael Faraday	Sir Isaac Newton
Enrico Fermi	Max Planck
Alexander Fleming	Joseph Priestley
Galileo	Ernest Rutherford
Galen	Matthias Schleiden
Yuri Gagarin	Theodor Schwann
William Harvey	Adam Smith
Hippocrates	Andrew Vesalius

THE SOLAR SYSTEM

Your students will learn more about the solar system in an exciting way, either individually or in groups.

Grade: six to eight

Duration: 30 to 40 minutes

Materials: *HyperStudio, HyperStudio* planning sheets

Before the Computer:

- If students are working in groups, they will need to meet and make assignments, including who will design the title page and which planets to research.
- Students will need to use an electronic encyclopedia or other resources to gather information on their topic.

On the Computer:

- Students will set up the title page "The Solar System" on the first card.
- The second card should display a graphic of the solar system. This card will act as the main menu or home card.
- Students will each make cards with their information in a text object.
- An invisible button will be placed on each planet, linking to the information about that planet.
- On the text card (the card with the information about each planet), a button will be added linking the card back to the solar system.
- On the home card, have an EXIT button to take the viewer to the last card which will be the credits card.
- On the credits card, place a Text Object and make it an invisible button and choose NBA, new button action, Roll Credits.

Hint:

If students are novices at computers and especially the *HyperStudio* program, have the students create all their cards first by selecting New Card. After all the blank cards are made, give a mini-lesson on buttons and linking cards.

A *HyperStudio* planning sheet has been filled out as an example. A blank, reproducible form appears in the Resources and Additional References section of this book.

SOLAR SYSTEM *(example)*

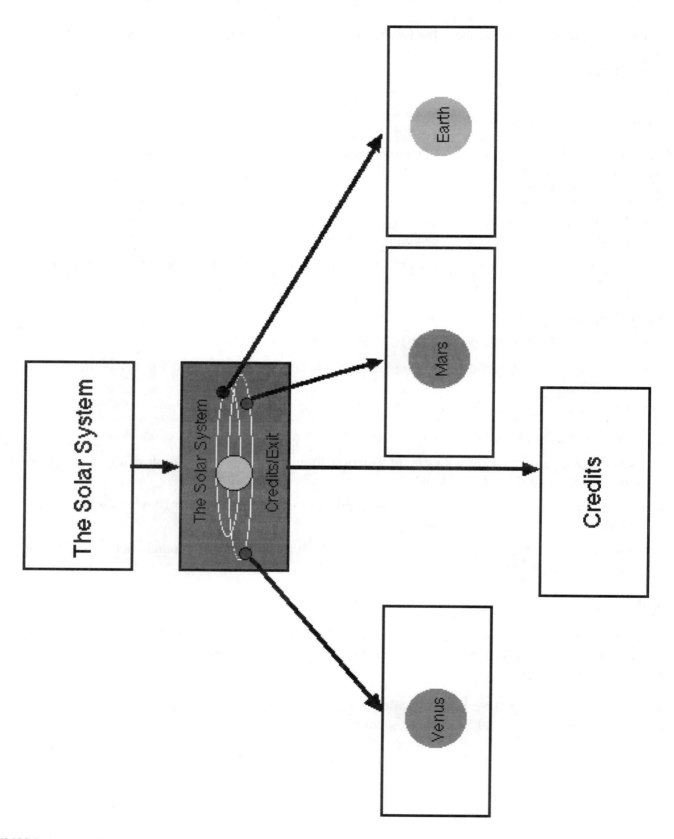

SCIENCE INTERNET SCAVENGER HUNT

Seach engines will get you around the World Wide Web and retrieve information about almost any subject, but how well do your students understand the difference between quantity information and quality information? Wax up your virtual surfboard and catch an Internet wave.

Grade level: six to eight

Duration: variable, depending on the number of links followed, speed of connection, etc.

Materials: access to Internet, Science Scavenger Hunt sheet

Before the Computer:

- Discuss the school's rules of the Internet. Remind them that they should only search the sites listed on the list.

- Review the URL addresses. (ex., gov is a government site, edu is an educational site)

- Answer any questions about the scavenger hunt. If you have one computer in the classroom, you may want to pair up students for this search.

On the Computer:

- Students will type in the URL address and search for the information. Answers will be recorded on the scavenger sheet.

The sites listed on the worksheet were appropriate and accurate at the time of this printing. However, it is a good idea to visit these sites before assigning the lesson. If a site has changed, you may want to look for alternative sites with similar themes.

SCIENCE SCAVENGER HUNT

The Toucan Sam Rain Forest Encyclopedia
http://www.toucansam.com

Name and describe two kinds of plants found in the rain forest.

1. _____

2. _____

The NASA Home Page
http://www.nasa.gov

Where can you order NASA photographs? _____

What link do you use if you are looking for information for a school paper? _____

_____

MTV Volcanoes Page—World Reference Map
http://www.geo.mtu.edu/volcanoes/world.html

Give the name and location of an active volcano for each of the following areas:

1. Southwest Pacific: _____

2. Southeast Asia:_____

3. India: _____

4. East Asia (Japan): _____

5. East Asia (Kamachatka): _____

6. North America: _____

7. North America: _____

8. North America: _____

THE OLYMPIC GAMES

Students will discover the history of the Olympics while learning about the various sports in the Olympic Games.

Grade level: six to eight

Duration: 20 to 30 minutes

Materials: *ClarisWorks,* Olympic information sheet, *ClarisWorks* planning sheet

Before the Computer:

- Students will be divided into a Summer Olympics group and Winter Olympics group.

- Each group will research a topic and decide on one sport in the Olympics to research.

- Students will research their sport, including information listed on the Olympic information sheet.

- Groups will meet and organize their presentation using the *ClarisWorks* planning sheet. (Suggestion: Students will want to present their research in chronological order.)

On the computer:

- Students can scan and save graphics or pictures to be used in their presentation.

- In *ClarisWorks,* students will select the word processing module.

- The group will be responsible for determining font, size, and style for the text.

- Students will take turns typing in their information.

After all information is entered, students will select slide show and select options for their presentation.

A *ClarisWorks* slide show planning sheet has been filled out as an example. A blank, reproducible form appears in the Resources and Additional References section of this book.

OLYMPIC INFORMATION SHEET

What sport did your group select? _____

_____

How is the sport played? What equipment (if any) is involved? _____

_____

_____

What year did the sport officially become an Olympic sport?_____

_____

Select two years the Olympic games were held and describe the following:

The first year we selected was _____

That year, the Olympic games were held in _____

Who won the medals in the sport for that year? What nation were they representing? _____

_____

_____

The second year we selected was _____

That year, the Olympic games were held in _____

Who won the medals in the sport for that year? What nation were they representing? _____

_____

_____

SYSTEMS OF THE BODY

The systems of the body will come alive as students create an interactive *HyperStudio* stack about the different systems of the body. If you do not have access to a lab so each student can work on an individual project, break the project into groups, assigning the different systems to each member of the group.

Grade level: six to eight

Duration: 30 to 40 minutes on computer

Materials: *HyperStudio*, *HyperStudio* planning sheet

Before the Computer:

- Introduce the project to the students.
- Have students use research materials to find information about the systems of the body and complete the planning sheet.
- Students will use *HyperStudio* planning sheets to organize their stack.

On the Computer:

- Students will create cards using their notes.
- They should include a title card and links from the home card to each system information card. If a scanner or clip art is available, have students link to a card with the system diagram or add graphic objects to their information card.
- Each information card in the stack should include a button to return to the home page.

Please see the example of the Solar System to see how a sample stack is organized.

A *HyperStudio* planning sheet has been filled out as an example. A blank, reproducible form appears in the Resources and Additional References section of this book.

SYSTEMS OF THE BODY

Name: _____   Date: _____

NERVOUS SYSTEM

Parts: _____

Function: _____

CIRCULATORY SYSTEM

Parts: _____

Function: _____

MUSCULAR SYSTEM

Parts: _____

Function: _____

DIGESTIVE SYSTEM

Parts: _____

Function: _____

RESPIRATORY SYSTEM

Parts: _____

Function: _____

SKELETAL SYSTEM

Parts: _____

Function: _____

SCIENCE FAIR PROJECT PRESENTATION

What better way for a student to organize and present their science fair project information than with a *HyperStudio* stack? By tracking the project from beginning to end, students will gain an insight into the process involved in tackling a large project.

Grade level: six to eight

Duration: 30 to 40 minutes on the computer

Materials: Science Fair Project summary sheet, *HyperStudio* planning sheet, *HyperStudio*

Before the Computer:

- As the students prepare and develop their science fair projects, students will use the summary sheet to record the information.

On the Computer:

- Students should begin their *HyperStudio* stacks before their science fair projects are complete.

- They can begin creating cards with a title page, their hypothesis, procedure, and materials and other information related to their experiment.

- Graphs can be made using *ClarisWorks* or an another other spreadsheet program and imported into a card for the stack.

- As each portion of the project is completed, a card may be added to the stack.

A *HyperStudio* planning sheet has been filled out as an example. A blank, reproducible form appears in the Resources and Additional References section of this book.

SCIENCE FAIR PROJECT

Student: _____   Date_____

Project Title: _____

Question: What do you want to find out?

_____

_____

Hypothesis: What do you think you will find out?

_____

_____

Materials: What is needed for the project?

_____

_____

_____

Procedure: How will you find out? List the steps.

_____

_____

_____

Results: What happened?

_____

_____

Conclusion: What did you learn?

_____

_____

TRACK YOUR PULSE

When studying the heart and the importance of exercise, your pulse rate plays an important part. With this project, students will begin to understand about the pulse rate.

Grade level: six to eight

Duration: 30 to 40 minutes on computer

Materials: planning sheet, stopwatch

Procedure:

Students can work in pairs or in groups.

Before the Computer:

- The class will discuss the heart and its functions, exercise/activities, and pulse rates.
- The techniques of taking the pulse and locations where the pulse of an individual can be taken using the finger and a stopwatch will be demonstrated by the teacher, and the students will practice.
- Students could research normal pulse rates and various pulse rates during different activities.
- The pulse of each individual will be taken prior to the activity and immediately after the activity with the results recorded on the planning sheet.

Three activities and participation time will be planned where the pulse rate will be taken and recorded using the stopwatch. (ex. Students will jump on one leg for 5 minutes or students will run one lap around the football field.)

On the Computer:

- Members of the group will enter data on the spreadsheet, choosing variables and type of graph.
- The group will make at least two graphs to compare the data, deciding which graph best displays their results.

TRACK YOUR PULSE *(cont.)*

GRAPH EXAMPLES

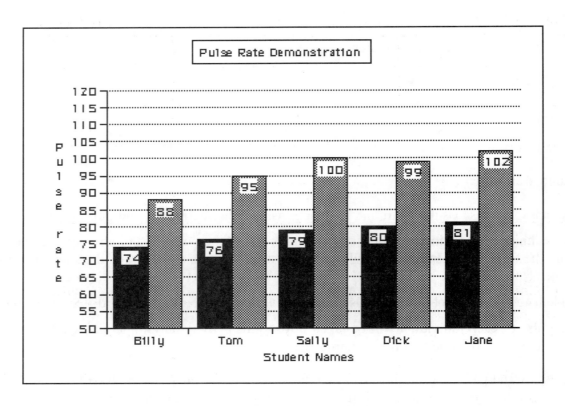

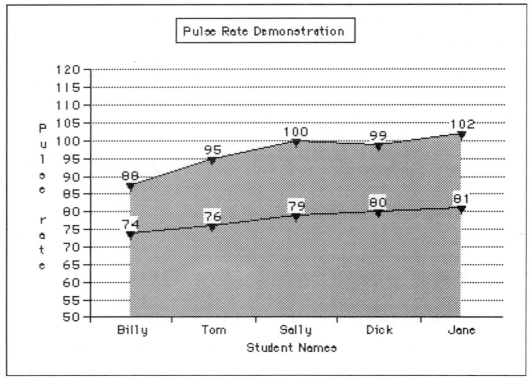

TRACK YOUR PULSE *(cont.)*

Group name _____

Activity _____

Members of Group	Beginning Pulse	Activity Pulse

Activity _____

Members of Group	Beginning Pulse	Activity Pulse

Activity _____

Members of Group	Beginning Pulse	Activity Pulse

COUNTRY/STATE STUDY

Students can be divided into groups or work independently to study a country or state selected from the textbook and design a multimedia presentation to share the information with the class.

Grade level: six to eight

Duration: 60 to 120 minutes on computer

Materials: fact sheet, *HyperStudio* planning worksheet

Students will research their country or state on an electronic encyclopedia and the Internet. Use a fact sheet to record information. When searching the Internet, students will search the country or state name plus tourism. (ex., "England tourism"). This will link students to areas where they can locate e–mail addresses or forms to complete to receive information. Students may use their correct name when requesting information but must give the school address.

Before the computer:

- Students will use an electronic encyclopedia and the Internet to research their country/state.
- Students will record information on the handout.
- Students will use a planning sheet to organize their presentation, writing captions and including possible graphics to be used.

On the Computer:

- Students will use the *HyperStudio* program to design a 10-card stack. Each student will be responsible for creating at least two cards in the stack.
- Students will select borders, background colors, buttons, and set other options.
- Students will scan and import pictures, if available, or import graphics from other sources such as the Internet.

Tip:

You may want to create a folder named graphics for students to download their graphics. Remind them to give specific names to their files so they can be easily identified.

COUNTRY STUDY

Name _____   Country _____

Country Fact Sheet

Capital: _____

Official language: _____

Form of government: _____

Head of government: _____

Chief products: _____

_____

_____

Area in square miles: _____

Map of country with surrounding countries:

[ ]

Flag:

[ ]

STATE STUDY

Name _____   State _____

State Fact Sheet

Capital: _____

Official language: _____

Form of government: _____

Head of government: _____

Chief products: _____

_____

_____

Area in square miles: _____

Map of country with surrounding countries:

```
┌─────────────────────────────────────────────────┐
│                                                   │
│                                                   │
│                                                   │
│                                                   │
│                                                   │
│                                                   │
│                                                   │
│                                                   │
└─────────────────────────────────────────────────┘
```

Flag:

```
┌─────────────────────────────────────────────────┐
│                                                   │
│                                                   │
│                                                   │
│                                                   │
│                                                   │
└─────────────────────────────────────────────────┘
```

THE WHITE HOUSE

Students will explore the White House and learn about the president of the United States and how he or she lives. This site will also introduce the students to our government.

Grade level: six to eight

Duration: 20 to 30 minutes

Materials: handout, Internet access

Before the Computer:

- Discuss the White House as being the home of the president of the United States and his or her family.
- Talk about the site you will be visiting. The site is maintained by the United States government.

On the Computer:

- Class will connect to the Internet and type in: http://www.whitehouse.gov
- Show the class how to bookmark a site.
- Students will use the handout and search the site to locate the answers.

Options:

Following the assignment, have students discuss their findings. Students should use the information to write a short article that can be used for the Using the Thesaurus project.

WHITE HOUSE
INTERNET SCAVENGER HUNT

Name: _____

List two accomplistments of the president:

1. _____

_____

_____

2. _____

_____

_____

List two accomplistments of the vice president:

1. _____

_____

_____

2. _____

_____

_____

What is the complete name of the first lady? _____

If the first family has a pet, write a sentence describing the pet:

_____

_____

TOURISM BROCHURE

Research skills, writing, design, geography, and creativity skills will be utilized to create a tourism brochure on a country/province from the text.

Grade level: six to eight

Duration: 30 to 40 minutes on the computer

Materials: *ClarisWorks*, planning sheet

Before the Computer:

- Create a brochure template in *ClarisWorks* ahead of time for the students to use.

- Assign or have the students choose a country from the text that they will be studying.

- Encourage your students to take notes and save to disk any pictures or graphics that can be used in their brochure.

- Provide students with a planning sheet so they can prepare for their time on the computer.

- Think of a catchy name for your brochure.

On the Computer:

- Students will use the template to type in their text and insert their graphics.

- Pictures, maps, and graphics can be scanned and saved to a disk or the hard drive.

- Students will save their work on a disk and print out a hard copy.

- To print, the students will need to print one page, insert the page back into the printer tray and print the back page. Another option would be to print pages separately and mount them on construction paper.

Examples of brochure names:

- Let's Visit Italy

- The Boot Country

- Experience the Wine Country

- Come to Italy

TOURISM BROCHURE *(cont.)*

Student Name: _____

Date: _____

Important Facts

Bibliography

TOURISM BROCHURE *(cont.)*

What to See

Map Including Points of Interests

EARLY NATIVE AMERICANS

Let your students share their research on Early Native Americans with the class through a slide show presentation.

Grade level: six to eight

Duration: 30 to 40 minutes on the computer

Materials: Early Native American worksheet, *ClarisWorks* slide show planning sheet

Before the Computer:

- Assign your students to research a Native American tribe or assign tribes to small groups.
- Have your students use research materials to answer the questions on the Early Native American Worksheet.
- Students will use a slide show planning sheet to plan their presentations.
- Give students the opportunity to evaluate their own work by providing them with the slide show checklist.

On the Computer:

- Students will use *ClarisWorks* to type in their information.
- Under View from the menu bar, select slide show.
- Select background options

Options:

Students can share their presentations as each Native American tribe is studied in the curriculum, or presentations may be delivered at the end of the unit.

A *ClarisWorks* slide show planning sheet has been filled out as an example. A blank, reproducible form appears in the Resources and Additional References section of this book.

EARLY NATIVE AMERICAN WORKSHEET

Student name: _____ Native American tribe: _____

Where was your tribe located? Were they relocated? When? To where?

_____

1. How did the Native American tribe meet their basic food needs?

_____

_____

2. How did the Native American tribe meet their basic shelter needs?

_____

_____

3. How did the Native American tribe meet their basic clothing needs?

_____

_____

4. What type of transportation was used by the Native American tribe?

_____

_____

5. What forms of art and architecture did the Native American tribe develop?

_____

_____

6. What forms of recreation did the Native American tribe develop?

_____

_____

7. What advancements in science did the Native American tribe provide?

_____

_____

SUPPORT PROGRAMS

Many middle schools offer students a choice of elective classes in addition to their regular class load of language arts, math, science, and social studies. When the school bell rings for these classes, you can see how the students spring to life as they head for the music room, the art room, a journalism class or a foreign language class. Quite often, the students have had an opprotunity to select the elective they are rushing off to participate in. It was their choice. It was their decision. And you can see how being able to make a choice in their own education empowers them.

These support programs are very important to the development of students. While a media specialist uses technology frequently in his or her instruction as a matter of course, other support personnel may not realize the importance of integrating technology into the curriculum. They may not even be aware of what resources are available to them, or they may not believe that their subject area can successfully incorporate technology as a learning component.

If your elective meets regularly, you should take advantage of all the time possible to use technology in your classroom instruction. The lessons that follow are an excellent way to get students involved and make use of the technology in your school. Request time to use the media center or computer lab for research.

If you are an itinerant support person (an individual who travels to more than one school to teach), inquire as to times you can use the media center for research using the reference books, electronic encyclopedias, or the Internet. If the school has a computer lab, ask for time slots you can use to develop student technology projects.

The following pages have suggestions for possible ways to implement a program using technologies available in the school. All lessons can be organized as either group activities or individual activities.

THE HISTORY OF ART IN WESTERN CULTURE

Students will gain an understanding of the development of art through this project. Art plays an important role in the development of the societies and cultures that developed.

Grade level: six to eight

Duration: 30 to 40 minutes on the computer

Materials: *ClarisWorks,* information sheet, *ClarisWorks* planning sheets

Before the Computer:

- The teacher assigns groups and topics for research.
- Using the information sheet, students will use available resources to research their topic.
- The *ClarisWorks* planning sheets will be used to plan at least eight slides. The first slide will include the title and student/group name.
- If a scanner is available, students can scan pictures to be used in the presentation.
- If students have access to the Internet, they can locate and save images to be used in their presentation.

On the Computer:

- Students will use the *ClarisWorks* word processing module to type in their information, inserting images saved from the scanner or Internet.
- Students should edit their documents, checking for spelling, grammatical errors, and coherence.
- From View in the menu, select Slide Show. Students will choose background color, transitions, and other options.
- Save to disk.

Options:

Students may use this to write a paragraph or story on art's influence on civilization. Another option would be to make posters, collages, or other artistic displays.

A *ClarisWorks* slide show planning sheet has been filled out as an example. A blank, reproducible form appears in the Resources and Additional References section of this book.

THE HISTORY OF ART IN WESTERN CULTURE *(cont.)*

4000–330 B.C.

Ancient Near Eastern Art

3200–3230 B.C.

Egyptian Art

2800–1100 B.C.

Aegean Art

1100–100 B.C.

Greek Art

700–741 B.C.

Etruscan Art

200 B.C.–330 A.D.

Roman Art

100–1453 A.D.

Early Christian and Byzantine Art

400–1400 A.D.

Medieval Art in the North

1400–1600 A.D.

Renaisssance Art

1600–1700 A.D.

Early Baroque Art

1700–1800 A.D.

Later Baroque
Rococo
Neoclassic Art

1800–1900 A.D.

Neoclassic to Post-Impressionist Art

1900 to present

Modern Art
Photography
Motion Pictures

THE HISTORY OF ART IN WESTERN CULTURE *(cont.)*

Group name: _____   Topic: _____

Briefly describe the characteristics of the period. _____

_____

_____

Who were the important artists during the period? _____

_____

_____

_____

Architecture: (describe) _____

_____

_____

Sculpture: (describe or list several important pieces)_____

_____

_____

_____

Paintings: (describe or list several important pieces)_____

_____

_____

_____

FAMOUS ARTISTS AND THEIR WORK

Students will gain an understanding of the development of art through this project. Art plays an important role in the development of the societies and cultures that developed.

Grade level: six to eight

Duration: 30 to 40 minutes on the computer

Materials: *HyperStudio*, biographical data sheet, *HyperStudio* planning sheet

Before the Computer:

- The Teacher assigns groups/individual artists for research.
- Using the information sheet, students will use available resources to research their artist.
- Students will use planning sheets to organize their presentation.
- If a scanner is available, students can scan pictures to be used in the presentation.
- If students have access to the Internet, they can locate and save pictures and photographs to be used in the presentation.

On the computer:

- Students will use *HyperStudio* to make cards for their stack using the planning sheets.
- Buttons should be placed on each card and import graphics scanned or saved off the Internet.
- Save to disk.

Options:

Students may use this information to write a paragraph or story on art's influence on civilization. Another option would be to make posters, collages, or other artistic displays.

A biographical data sheet has been filled out as an example. A blank, reproducible form appears in the Resources and Additional References section of this book.

A *HyperStudio* planning sheet has been filled out as an example. A blank, reproducible form appears in the Resources and Additional References section of this book.

FAMOUS ARTISTS

Ivan Albright	Jacques Lipchitz
George Bellows	Edouard Manet
George Bingham	Michelangelo
Milton Caniff	Claude Monet
Paul Cezanne	Edvard Munch
Marc Chagall	Barnett Newman
Leonardo Da Vinci	Pablo Picasso
Albrecht Durer	Pierre Auguste Renior
Francisco Goya	Peter Paul Rubens
Oskar Kokoschka	John Singer Sargent
Fernand Leger	

MUSICAL INSTRUMENTS

Students will gain an understanding of musical instruments through this project. Music played an important role in the development of societies and cultures. Music is also thought to increase intelligence when introduced at an early age.

Grade level: six to eight

Duration: 30 to 40 minutes on the computer

Materials: information sheet, *ClarisWorks* planning sheets

Before the Computer:

- The teacher assigns groups or individual instruments for research.
- Using the information sheet, students will use available resources to research their topic.
- The *ClarisWorks* planning sheets will be used to plan at least four or five slides (or whatever the teacher feels necessary). The first slide will include the title and student/group name.
- If a scanner is available, students can scan pictures to be used in the presentation.
- If students have access to the Internet, locate and save pictures and photographs to be used in the presentation.

On the Computer:

- Students will use the *ClarisWorks* word processing module to type in their information, inserting graphics or pictures saved from the scanner or Internet.
- From View in the menu, select slide show. Students will choose background color, transitions, and other options.
- Save to disk.

Options:

Students could have local musicians come to demonstrate their instruments. The class could go on a field trip to a concert.

If your computer supports sound, you could download musical pieces through the Internet.

MUSICAL INSTRUMENTS

Group/individual name(s): _____   Instrument:_____

What kind of instrument is this (example: string, wind, percussion) ? _____

_____

When was the instrument first invented? _____

_____

When did it become popular?_____

_____

What historical musicians or composers have used this instrument in their compositions?

_____

_____

What modern musicians or composers have used this instrument in their compositions?

_____

_____

Find at least two musical compositions that were written specifically for this instrument. Who wrote

them?_____

_____

When? _____

_____

Why do you think the composer chose this instrument over another? _____

_____

_____

INSTRUMENTS AND THEIR FAMILIES

STRINGED INSTRUMENTS

Banjo	Classical Guitar	Mandolin
Bass	Harp	Viola
Cello	Lute	Violin

BRASS INSTRUMENTS

Bugle	French Horn	Trombone
Flugelhorn	Sousaphone	Trumpet

WOODWIND INSTRUMENTS

Bass Clarinet	English Horn	Piccolo
Bassoon	Flute	Soprano Saxophone
Clarinet	Oboe	Tenor Saxophone

PERCUSSION INSTRUMENTS

Bass Drum	Cymbals	Snare Drum
Bongo Drums	Gong	Triangle
Chimes	Kettle Drum	Vibraphone

KEYBOARD INSTRUMENTS

Harpsichord	Piano	Pipe Organ

FAMOUS MUSICIANS/COMPOSERS AND THEIR WORK

Students will gain an understanding of the development of music through this project. Music played an important role in the development of societies and cultures.

Grade level: six to eight

Duration: 30 to 40 minutes on the computer

Materials: *HyperStudio*, biographical data sheet, *HyperStudio* planning sheet

Before the computer:

- Teacher assigns groups/individuals and musicians for research.
- Using the information sheet, students will use available resources to research their topic.
- Students will use planning sheet to organize their presentation.
- If scanner is available students can scan pictures to be used in the presentation.
- If students have access to the Internet, locate and save pictures and photographs to be used in the presentation.

On the computer:

- Students will use the *HyperStudio* to make cards for their stack using the planning sheets.
- Buttons should be placed on each card and import graphics scanned or saved off the Internet.
- Save to disk.

FAMOUS MUSICIANS/COMPOSERS

Henry Purcell
English

Antonia Vivaldi
Italian

Jean Philippe Rameau
French

Johann Sebastian Bach
German

George Frideric Handel
German

Joseph Haydn
Austrian

Wolfgang Amadeus Mozart
Austrian

Gioacchino Rossini
Italian

Franz Schubert
Austrian

Felix Mendelssohn
German

Frederic Chopin
Polish

Robert Schumann
German

Franz Liszt
Hungarian

Richard Wagner
German

Giuseppe Verdi
Italian

Cesar Franck
Belgian

Anton Bruckner
Austrian

Alexander Borodin
Russian

Johannes Brahms
German

Modest Mussorgsky
Russian

Peter Tchaikovsky
Russian

Claude Debussy
French

Richard Strauss
German

Arnold Schonberg
Austrian

Alban Berg
Austrian

Darius Milhaud
French

Aaron Copland
American

Gian Carlo Menotti
American

ELECTRONIC JOURNAL

Students will keep an electronic journal recording their thoughts and feelings of specific topics. This activity will give students an opportunity to use the computer to keep a journal while learning a word processing program, editing, and saving.

Grade level: six to eight

Duration: a few minutes on computer through the school year

Materials: formatted floppy disk for each student

Procedure:

Before the Computer:

- Distribute a formatted floppy disk to each student.
- Discuss privacy issues; for example, students do not boot up disks that belong to other students.
- Decide on the times the computer will be available for journal entries. If you have access to a lab, let students know which day you will be making journal entries.

On the Computer:

- Students will use *ClarisWorks* to make their journal entries, saving their work on the floppy disk.

Activities:

Students should be directed in their journal entries to record their thoughts and reactions to class-related topics. This protects the students and the teacher against any invasion of privacy issues when journals are evaluated. If the journals are to be evaluated for content, make the students aware of this ahead of time.

SOFTWARE EVALUATION AND SELECTION

To truly integrate technology into the middle school curriculum, the teacher has to choose the software for the classroom with an eye to its integrated use. "There is so much educational software available today; how do I choose the correct one for my class?" asks the middle school teacher in a confused voice. In the following pages, we hope to alleviate that confusion by offering criteria to use when evaluating and selecting software. Included in this section is a software evaluation form you might want to use when selecting software.

CATEGORIES OF SOFTWARE

Productivity—word processing, spreadsheets, and authoring

Creativity and Presentation—drawing, painting, making music or sounds, and multimedia

Tutorial—teaches material in an interactive way; decides when student has completed enough tasks to proceed to next level

Simulation—presents situations where the student makes decisions as if confronted with the real-life situation

Drill and Practice—provides practice in skills students have previously been taught

Problem Solving—uses critical thinking skills; not relegated to any specific content area

Games—specific learning objectives with the game serving as a motivational device; also referred to as edutainment

Telecommunications—allows the use of the Internet

SOFTWARE SELECTION

According to Dr. Vicki Sharp in her book *Computer Education for Teachers*, there are eight steps to be used in choosing good software.

1. Know the specific software needs of the population—grade level, ability, purpose of software, class language, needs.

2. Locate the software—educational software catalogs, preview centers, magazines, demo copies from the publishers, reviews, software stores.

3. Research hardware compatibility—memory requirements, hardware requirements (e.g., CD-ROM player needed, graphics card needed, etc).

4. Examine the program's contents—appropriateness for students, use evaluation form (page 148).

5. Look at instructional design—learner control, reinforcement, sequencing, flexibility, appearance.

6. Check to see how easily the program is learned—easy to learn, simple commands, adequate help on screen and in manuals.

7. Evaluate the program in terms of consumer value—lab packs, site licenses.

8. Investigate the technical support and cost—toll-free number for help, return policy.

SOFTWARE EVALUATION AND SELECTION *(cont.)*

Educational Software Packaging

There are several ways in which educational software is packaged for school use:

Home Version-Consumer Version—includes one disk/CD and no teaching materials.

School Version—includes disks/CD and a teacher's manual which usually includes online and offline classroom material for use with the program. Most have lesson plans, templates, and overhead masters. This package is usually for use on one computer only.

Lab Pack—usually includes five disks/CDs and teacher classroom materials. Some lab packs are available with ten or more disks/CDs. The price makes this a good school purchase for 5, 10, or 15 computers.

Site License—means permission is granted for legally copying the program for every computer in a specific building, school or district. It includes teacher classroom materials and is a good choice for schools with many computers. Some site licenses are for an unlimited number of copies; however, others are for a specific number.

Network Version—indicates the program has been specifically formatted so it can be installed on the network and shared with all of the networked computers.

SOFTWARE EVALUATION CHECKLIST

Program Title: _____ Publisher: _____

Grade Level: _____ Subject Area: _____

Version: _____ Evaluation Date: _____

Documentation	**Disagree**				**Agree**
Hardware requirements are clearly stated.	1	2	3	4	5
Installation is easy to follow.	1	2	3	4	5
Goals/objectives are clearly defined.	1	2	3	4	5
Additional activities are provided.	1	2	3	4	5
Prerequisite skills are stated.	1	2	3	4	5
Operation of Software					
Instructions are age appropriate.	1	2	3	4	5
Help screens are available.	1	2	3	4	5
The screen display is appealing to students.	1	2	3	4	5
The student controls the pace.	1	2	3	4	5
The student can exit the software at any time.	1	2	3	4	5
The student can re-enter the program where stopped.	1	2	3	4	5
It has long-term interest.	1	2	3	4	5
Presentation					
It is age appropriate.	1	2	3	4	5
Sounds enhance the program.	1	2	3	4	5
Graphics are appropriate.	1	2	3	4	5
Positive reinforcement is appropriate.	1	2	3	4	5
Negative reinforcement is appropriate.	1	2	3	4	5
Content					
Content is accurate.	1	2	3	4	5
Biases/stereotypes are in the content.	1	2	3	4	5
It fills a unique need.	1	2	3	4	5
Content is presented in a variety of ways.	1	2	3	4	5
Management					
A student management system is available.	1	2	3	4	5
There are clear reports for student achievement.	1	2	3	4	5
Student records are private.	1	2	3	4	5
Records are easily accessible by teachers.	1	2	3	4	5

Hardware: _____ Printer compatibility: _____

Memory needed: _____ Installation requirements: _____

Platform: _____ Peripherals needed: _____

Recommendation

Excellent   Good   Poor

HYPERSTUDIO

Tools:

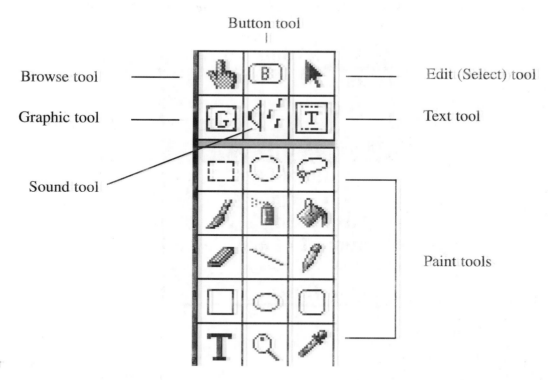

Button tool

Browse tool ——— ——— Edit (Select) tool

Graphic tool ——— ——— Text tool

Sound tool

Paint tools

Menu Bar

All of these pulldown menus help you navigate and create in your stack.

 File   Edit   Move   Tools   Objects   Colors   Options   Extras

Quick Tips:

Command-S—Saves your stack (File Menu)

Command-B—Adds a button (Objects Menu)

Command-G—Adds a graphic item (Objects Menu)

Command-T—Adds a text box (Objects Menu)

Command-L—Adds a movie or video (Objects Menu)

Command-N—Creates a new card (Edit Menu)

Painting Your Card:

• Choose a background color for your card/stack. You do not have to have one, but it adds interest.

• Add clip art from the file menu; it allows you to add graphics from a disk onto your card.

• New card (Command-N) in the edit menu creates a new, blank card following the current one. You can use ready made cards that have neat backgrounds and are already in the edit menu.

HYPERSTUDIO *(cont.)*

The move menu helps you navigate around your stack before you have created all of your buttons.

```
Move   Tools   Objects
   Back              ⌘~
   Home              ⌘H

   First Card        ⌘1
   Previous Card     ⌘<
   Next Card         ⌘>
   Last Card         ⌘9
   Jump To Card...   ⌘J

   Find Text...      ⌘F
```

Adding Objects to Your Card:

The object menu helps you add text, buttons, movies, etc., to your stack. For example, just go to add a button in the object menu to add a navigational or effect button. The program will then lead you through the steps to make your button work. The same goes for text, graphic items, movies, and sounds.

```
Objects   Colors   Options   Ex
   Item Info...        ⌘I
   Card Info...
   Background Info...
   Stack Info...

   Bring Closer        ⌘+
   Send Farther        ⌘-

   Add a Button...     ⌘B
   Add a Graphic Item... ⌘G
   Add a Text Item...  ⌘T
   Add a Movie or Video... ⌘L
```

Each time you add a new object to your card, *HyperStudio* will lead you through the necessary steps (selecting style, placement, actions, etc.) to make your object work.

Check Out Your Stack:

Extras—Storyboard is a great way to get an overview of your stack. Using this option you can look at all the cards in your stack, rearrange them, and delete them if necessary.

THE WRITING CENTER

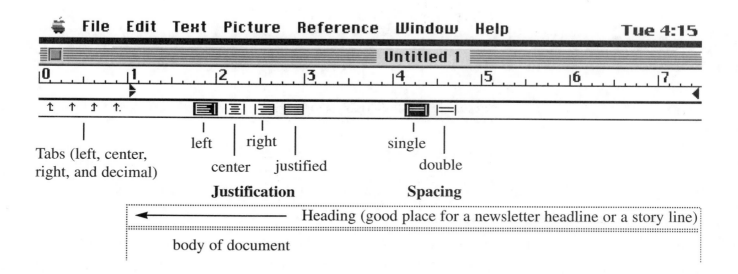

File

This allows you to do major functions that affect your whole document, such as save, print, create a new document, change your margins, quit, etc.

Edit

You can copy and paste, change your preferences, change spacing, etc.

Text

Here is where you change the way your letters look.

Picture

This menu lets you select pictures, change their sizes, crop them, rotate and flip pictures, and even give them borders.

Reference

This checks spelling and gives you access to the thesaurus.

Window

It shows you what is on your clipboard and allows you to move between open documents.

Help

This gives you additional information about the menu bar function you are using.

THE WRITING CENTER *(cont.)*

Creating Documents

When you double-click on the program, you will get a dialogue box that looks like this.

Report or Letter: Create a normal document with a body; you choose if you want a heading.

Newsletter: Create a document with two columns and a heading.

Custom: Set up a document by orientation (page setup), number of columns, and choice of heading.

Select the type of document you wish to create. If you are opening something you have already created and saved, click on Open Saved Document.

When you go to New in the File menu while working in *The Writing Center,* you will get the same dialogue box.

Setting Margins

The Writing Center automatically sets 1" (2.5 cm) margins all the way around your document. If you wish to change these margins, go to Page Setup in the File menu. Use the tab key to take you to Margin Settings. Press delete to delete 1" (2.5 cm). Type in the margins you need (e.g., $\frac{1}{2}$" [1.25 cm] would be .5). Press OK.

Changing the Text Style

To change the way your letters look, go to Font in the Text menu. Here you can set the font, text style, and point size. You may set the text style for the entire document before you begin typing or change it in parts as you go by selecting the text you want to change.

Important Note: When you are working with a heading, that text is separate, so you must change it separately. What you select in the body of your document will not affect your heading and vice versa.

Adding a Picture

Go to Picture—Choose a Picture. There is a folder in *The Writing Center* folder called Pictures. It has pictures for you to choose from in many categories. Select the category you need (Animals, Nature/Science, School, etc.) and click Open Folder. Find the picture you need and select Place in Document. Use the Picture pulldown menu to make any necessary changes to your picture. (You can also bring in your own pictures with Choose a Picture.)

CLARISWORKS 4.0

Creating a *ClarisWorks* Word Processing Document

Double-click on *ClarisWorks*. If the application is open, go to New in the File menu.

Select the type of document you want to produce—Word Processing.

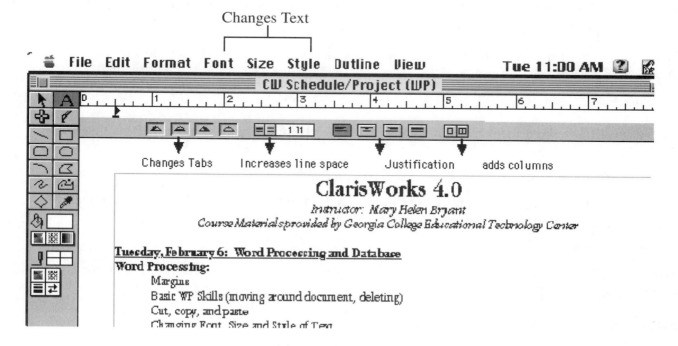

To change margins select Format from the Document menu.

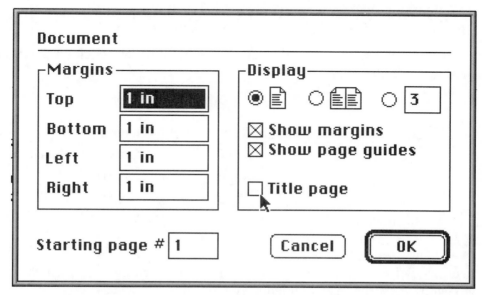

The default margins are set at 1" (2.5 cm). In order to change them, select Document from the Format menu. When the document dialog box appears, you can type in the measurements you need (e.g., half-inch margins are set at .5). Use the tab to move from top to bottom and right to left.

CLARISWORKS 4.0 *(cont.)*

Moving Around Your Document

There are two ways in which you can move around within your word processing document.

— You can use the mouse to move around within your word processing document.

— You can use the arrow keys to move around within your word processing document.

Changing Text Font, Size, and Style

When you want or need to change a font, point size, and/or style, you need to follow three easy steps.

1. Use the mouse to highlight the desired text you wish to change.

2. Select Font, Size, and/or Format.

      a. In the Font menu you can choose Times, Helvetica, or any number of fonts that are available.

      b. In the Size menu you can choose any number between 4 and 255.

      c. In the Style menu you can choose a variety of text styles (e.g., bold, italics, underline, plain text, etc.). You can also use keyboard shortcuts to change styles.

Cut, Copy, and Paste

When you want or need to cut, copy, and/or paste a section of text, you need to follow four easy steps.

1. Use the mouse to highlight the desired text you wish to cut or copy.

2. Select Cut or Copy from the Edit menu.

3. Move your cursor to the place where you wish to insert the cut or copied text.

4. Select Paste from the Edit menu.

Tabs

There are four different types of tabs—Left, Center, Right, and Decimal.

In order to change tabs, which are automatically set at .5" (1.25 cm) left, click on the desired tab and drag it to the desired point on the ruler.

Example:

Left Tab	Center Tab	Right Tab	Decimal Tab
Student	Teacher	Grade	Supply Donation
Patrice Scott	Jones	Seventh	$1.50
Blake Atkins	Loeber	Fifth	$.50
Jenny Bavaro	Buffington	Sixth	$12.00

Writing Tools

• Spelling Checker—Select Check Document Spelling from Writing Tools, which is in the Edit menu. (The keyboard shortcut is Command =.)

• Thesaurus—Highlight the word you wish to change and then select Thesaurus from Writing Tools, which is in the Edit menu. (The keyboard shortcut is Shift Command Z.)

CLARISWORKS 4.0 *(cont.)*

CLARISWORKS SPREADSHEET

Creating a Graph

1. Double-click on the *ClarisWorks* application.

2. Select Spreadsheet and then click OK.

3. On the screen you will see the rows and columns of your spreadsheet. Begin by typing your information into cell address A1. The information you type will appear in the data entry box but will not be entered into the cell address until you press the return key or enter key. If you have made a mistake in a cell you have already entered, select the cell with the error and retype it. The new version will not appear until you press return or enter.

	File	**Edit**	**Format**	**Calculate**	**Options**	**View**

Untitled 1 (SS)

B4   × ✓ 1

	A	**B**	**C**	**D**	
1	How I Spend My Day	#of hours			
2	sleeping	8			
3	working	10			
4	cooking	1			
5	reading	0.5			
6	eating	1			
7	playing/resting	4.5			
8					
9					
10					
11					
12					

4. In column A, type what you want to measure. For example, if you were going to graph favorite foods, this column would contain the different types (e.g., pizza, tacos, hamburgers, etc.). To move from cell to cell, you can use your mouse or your arrow keys. If your entries are too large to fit into your column, place your cursor at the end of the column header cells (A, B, C, etc.). When the arrow turns into a cursor, you will be able to increase the size of your columns. You can do the same thing with row sizes.

5. In column B, type your measurements. For example, if you were graphing favorite foods, this column would contain the number of votes each food received. Only numbers should be entered into this column.

6. Click and drag your mouse across all of the information you entered until everything is highlighted.

CLARISWORKS 4.0 *(cont.)*

CLARISWORKS SPREADSHEET *(cont.)*

7. Select Make Chart from the Options menu. It will give you a general menu that looks like this:

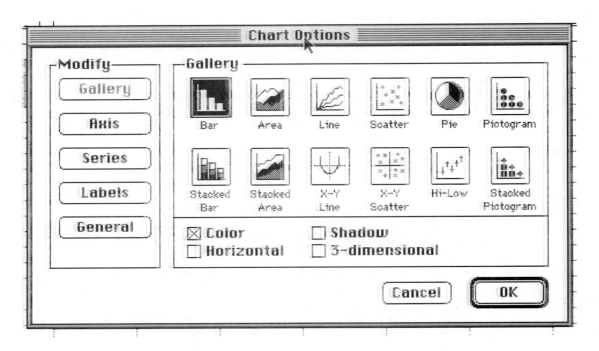

8. Select the type of graph you would like (e.g., pie, bar, etc.) and click OK.

9. To add or change a title, select Modify Chart from the Options menu and then click on labels. Axes (labels x and y axis), Series (changes appearance), Labels (adds titles, etc.), and General offers options that allow you to add or change things to your graph.

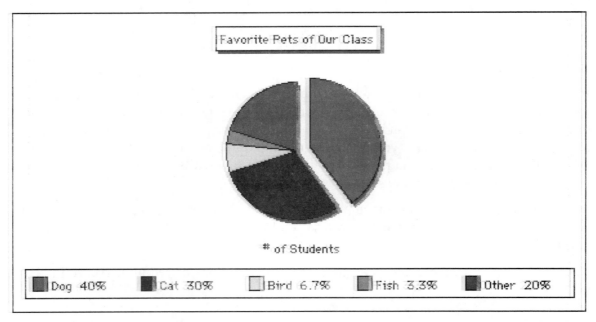

CLARISWORKS 4.0 *(cont.)*

CLARISWORKS SPREADSHEET *(cont.)*

Performing Calculations in *ClarisWorks* Spreadsheet

ClarisWorks can perform calculations for you automatically with just a few simple steps:

1. Set up your spreadsheet.

	A	B
1	Expense	Cost
2		
3	Pens	$6.50
4	Pencils	$2.20
5	Paper	$13.22
6	Diskettes	$33.25
7	Ribbons	$9.85
8		
9	Total	
10		
11	Average Expense	
12	Minimum	
13	Maximum	
14		

To set your number specifications (currency, decimals, etc.), highlight the cells you want to format and select Number from the Format menu. Click on the desired number format and then click OK.

Format Number, Date, and Time

Number
- ○ General
- ● Currency
- ○ Percent
- ○ Scientific
- ○ Fixed

- ☐ Commas
- ☐ Negatives in ()

Precision **2**

Date
- ○ 11/29/94
- ○ Nov 29, 1994
- ○ November 29, 1994
- ○ Tue, Nov 29, 1994
- ○ Tuesday, November 29, 1994

Time
- ○ 5:20 PM   ○ 17:20
- ○ 5:20:15 PM   ○ 17:20:15

[Cancel]   [OK]

CLARISWORKS 4.0 *(cont.)*

CLARISWORKS SPREADSHEET *(cont.)*

Performing Calculations in *ClarisWorks* Spreadsheet (cont.)

2. To add all of the numbers in one column, highlight where you want the total to appear. Then, type in =SUM(cells to total). For example, the above formula would be=SUM(B3..B7). *ClarisWorks* will automatically enter the cell addresses if you click and drag across the desired cells.

   - **Note:** *ClarisWorks* formulas will not work without the = sign.

3. To find the average, minimum, and maximum values, use these functions:

   =AVERAGE(cells)   =MIN(cells)   =MAX(cells)

   To use a formula over and over again in the same row or column:

   If you are creating a spreadsheet for multiple people or months, you may need to reuse your formulas. Instead of retyping them every time, select Fill Right from the CALCULATE menu to go across or select Fill Down from the CALCULATE menu to go down.

Adding Borders

First, highlight the row header for the row you wish to give a border.

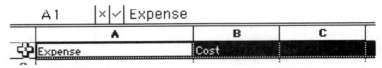

Second, the entire row should now be highlighted.

Third, select Borders from the Format menu. It will allow you to choose the part of the cell you wish to border. Select the desired border and click OK.

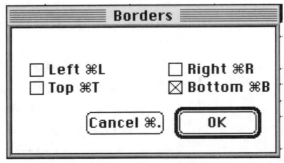

The row you highlighted should now have a solid line across the bottom.

	A	B	C	D	E
1	Expense	Cost			
2					
3	Pens	$6.50			
4	Pencils	$2.20			
5	Paper	$13.22			

HELPFUL FORMS AND PLANNING SHEETS

Once your students become comfortable being well-organized planners, they can use their own paper to plan. Until then, provide them with these guidelines for their technology projects.

Slide Show Storyboard

Use this form to plan for any type of slide show presentation. Copy the storyboard, front and back, for your students. Use as many sheets as necessary.

***HyperStudio* Planning Sheet**

Help students create *HyperStudio* stacks with this versatile planning sheet.

***HyperStudio* Planning Web**

Use these webs to help your students plan the organization and links of their *HyperStudio* presentation.

Biographical Data Sheet

Use this sheet to gather information about individuals students are researching.

***Writing Center* Planning Sheet**

Give your students the opportunity to arrange text and illustration in advance for a publishing project.

Status of the Class Project

Using this class list you can manage the progress of your students in any technology project.

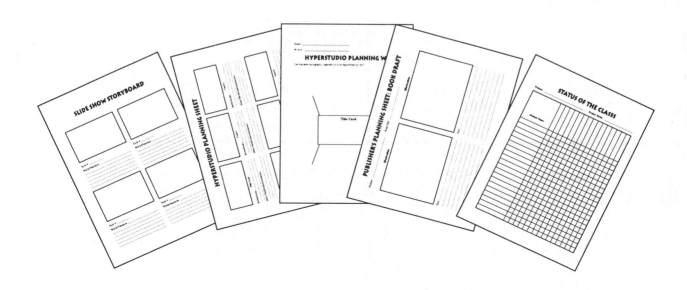

SLIDE SHOW STORYBOARD

Slide # _____

Words/Narration _____

_____

_____

_____

_____

_____

Slide # _____

Words/Narration _____

_____

_____

_____

_____

_____

Slide # _____

Words/Narration _____

_____

_____

_____

_____

_____

Slide # _____

Words/Narration _____

_____

_____

_____

_____

_____

HYPERSTUDIO PLANNING SHEET

Title Card

Buttons/Links: _____

Notes (Text/Sounds/Animations): _____

Card 1

Buttons/Links: _____

Notes (Text/Sounds/Animations): _____

Card 2

Buttons/Links: _____

Notes (Text/Sounds/Animations): _____

Card 3

Buttons/Links: _____

Notes (Text/Sounds/Animations): _____

Card 4

Buttons/Links: _____

Notes (Text/Sounds/Animations): _____

Card 5

Buttons/Links: _____

Notes (Text/Sounds/Animations): _____

Name: _____

Project: _____

HYPERSTUDIO PLANNING WEB

Use this sheet as a graphic organizer for your *HyperStudio* project.

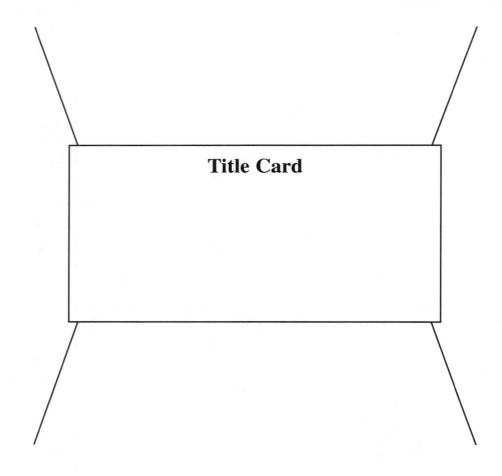

Title Card

BIOGRAPHICAL DATA SHEET

Student Name _____　　Due _____

Research Topic _____

INFORMATION TO RESEARCH AND RECORD

Date of birth:　　　　　　　　_____

Date of death (if applicable):　　_____

Place of birth:　　　　　　　　_____

Early life: _____

_____

Education: _____

_____

_____

Marriage/Family: _____

_____

_____

Major contributions/accomplishments:_____

_____

_____

Other information: _____

_____

_____

WRITING CENTER PLANNING SHEET

Student: _____

Book Title: _____

Illustration

Illustration

Text: _____

Text: _____

STATUS OF THE CLASSS

Project: _____   **Project Dates:** _____

Student Name													

SOFTWARE BIBLIOGRAPHY AND PURCHASE INFORMATION

ClarisWorks 4.0

ClarisWorks 4.0. Available from Claris Corporation. Claris Corporation, 5201 Patrick Henry Drive, Santa Clara, CA 95052.   1-800-544-8554.

ClarisWorks 4.0 is an integrated software package that combines word processing, drawing, painting, spreadsheets, database, and communications capabilities. There are no limits to the ways it can be used in the classroom for student and teacher productivity.

Teacher Note: Your school may already have software that will work well with the lesson plans in this book.

EasyBook

EasyBook. Available from Sunburst. Sunburst, 101 Castleton Street, P.O. Box 100, Pleasantville, NY 10570-0100. 1-800-321-7511.

This is an enjoyable and easy way to help your students become published authors. *EasyBook* makes it simple for students to publish and illustrate their own writings.

HyperStudio 3.0

HyperStudio 3.0. Available from Roger Wagner Publishing. Roger Wagner Publishing, Inc., 1050 Pioneer Way, Suite P, El Cajon, California 92020. 1-800-421-6526.

HyperStudio is recommended for the ultimate in multimedia presentations. This program is easy to use and has dialogue boxes that appear throughout to help you create your projects, including graphics, sound, text, *QuickTime* movies, and video.

The Writing Center

The Writing Center. Available from The Learning Company. The Learning Company, 6493 Kaiser Drive, Fremont, CA 94555. 1-800-852-2255.

This word processing/writing program is basic but very easy for students and teachers to use. The educational version comes with templates and sample projects for educational purposes.

OTHER SOFTWARE RESOURCES

Davidson and Associates
19840 Pioneer Ave.
Torrance, CA 90503
(800) 545-7677

Discis Knowledge Research, Inc.
P.O. Box 66
Buffalo, NY 14223-0066
(800) 567-4321

Edmark
P.O. Box 3218
Redmond, WA 98073-3218
(800) 426-0856

EduQuest/IBM
One Culver Road
Dayton, NJ 08810-9988
(800) 426-3327

Grolier Electronic Publishing
Sherman Turnpike
Danbury, CT 06816
(800) 356-5590

Lawrence Productions
1800 South 35th Street
Galesburg, MI 49053
(616) 665-7075

MECC
6160 Summit Drive North
Minneapolis, MN 55430-4003
(800) 685-6322

Microsoft Corproation
One Microsoft Way
Redmond, WA 98052
(800) 426-9400

National Geographic Educational Software
P.O. Box 98018
Washington, D.C. 20090-8018
(800) 368-2728

Scholastic, Inc.
2931 East McCarty Street
P.O. Box 7502
Jefferson City, MO 65102-9968
(800) 541-5513

Tom Snyder Productions
80 Coolidge Hill Road
Watertown, MA 02172
(800) 342-0236

Troll Associates
100 Corporate Drive
Mahwah, NJ 07498-0025
(800) 526-5289

WRITING GRANTS

PLANNING

Before any of that wonderful grant money comes rolling in, there is a certain amount of legwork that has to be done. The very first step is in identifying the *need* for the grant. It is usually much easier and more beneficial to discover what needs to be funded, rather than looking for funds and attempting to produce a need based on available money. It is is particularly important to use this approach for the following reasons:

- Gain the support of faculty, staff, and parents by addressing a universally perceived need.
- Gain the ideological support of the funder, who is more likely to fund a like-minded institution than one whose proposal is based on solely the availability of money.
- Gain momentum from programs already in place which could benefit from further funding.

Build a Team

The most important asset in writing a grant is the team of people who will take the grant from its planning stages through its execution and, when the grant money becomes available, to the final implementation of the funded program. This committee would ideally consist of the principal, teachers, parents, and other members of the community.

Once the committee has formed, members should be assigned permanent roles. The following roles represent the ideal grant writing team.

- **The Chairperson**—the person in charge of coordinating the committee's activities
- **Researchers**—members responsible for finding information on available grants and the grant writing process
- **Statisticians**—members who compile and gather data to be used in the grant proposal, including demographics, test profiles, test scores, etc.
- **Writer**—one person who is in charge of actually writing the grant (There should only be one writer so that the proposal maintains a consistent style.)
- **Editor**—at least one in addition to the writer to read and edit the proposal for content, grammar, punctuation, spelling, and sentence structure
- **Critic**—one person whose sole responsibility is to guard against bias being displayed in the proposal
- **Liaison**—the member who acts a liaison with other groups—business organizations, service clubs, parent organizations, etc.

Identify Needs

Determine what problems exist and what programs need to be initiated or expanded. For the purposes of writing the proposal, only select needs which can be addressed and solved by the grant. Collect supporting data to prove that the need does exist and that a solution is possible.

PLANNING*(cont.)*

Identify Funding Sources

After the intitial planning has been completed, it is time to look for sources of funding. Visit a Foundation Center, subscribe to the funding newsletters, read all of the articles. Consider alternative funding sources, such as parent groups, class donations, etc. Once you have found a grant that fits the need, it is time to start writing!

Identify Solutions

Describe what will be accomplished when the need is addressed. The objectives need to be stated as measurable outcomes which identify who is affected, a time frame, and criteria for measuring objectives.

WRITING THE GRANT PROPOSAL

While writing a grant may seem intimidating at first, all that is necessary to overcome the initial terror of facing a blank proposal is becoming familiar with the process. Below are some things to keep in mind while writing the proposal.

- **Follow the directions**. The directions for most grant proposals are *very* specific and should be follwed *exactly.*

- **Use the critics**. The writing must be extremely clear. Have the critics read and re-read everything until the document is completely clear. It might be a good idea to enlist people not on the committee for a cold read of the proposal.

- **Grammar and spelling are important**. Edit and proofread the proposal meticulously. Double-check homonyms, apostrophes, and possessives. Do not use contractions at all.

- **Number the pages**. If allowed or required to do so, make sure every page is numbered.

- **Keep a hard copy of everything**. Clearly mark drafts with the date and, if necessary, the time. Immediately replace old pages with new ones and discard the old pages so everyone has a current document. Try not to share the document electronically as this increases the chances of multiple versions.

- **When in doubt, call the funder**. If a question arises about any aspect of the proposal, call the funder for clarification.

Learn the Grant Elements

The various elements of the grant may have different names, depending on the specific proposal. The following terms are followed by brief definitions.

- **Title**—The title of the project should call attention to the proposal and not be cutesy. When referred to within the proposal, it should be highlighted in some fashion.

- **Abstract (Summary)**—This statement gives a synopsis of the whole grant proposal. Each section of the proposal should be represented in the abstract. It should be no longer than one page.

- **Table of Contents**—It should list the main sections of the grant in the order they are presented, with page numbers.

WRITING THE GRANT PROPOSAL *(cont.)*

- **Introduction**—It should identify the grant applicant, describe the purpose and goals of the project being proposed, and establish credibility.

- **Goal/Vision/Mission Statement**—This is the statement of ideals that most clearly defines the philosophy of the institution proposing the project. This is a good place to point out similarities between the philosophy of the funder and the applicant. This kind of statement is more general and is not measurable.

- **Statement of Needs (Problem)**—This is where the need or problem is explained. This is not a request for anything *needed*; it is a description of the current situation.

- **Objectives**—This describes what the situation will be after the implementation of the proposed project. This must be stated in measurable terms. It should include outcomes, who will do what, and when it will be done.

- **Activities**—This also known as methods, methodologies, strategies, and procedures. These are the steps that will be taken to achieve the desired results, to meet the objectives.

- **Management**—This explains how the project will be managed and who will be responsible for managing it. Names and titles of the people who will implement the project go here.

- **Personnel**—This section of the proposal profiles the important personnel connected with the project, including training, leadership qualifications, and related experience.

- **Time Lines**—The time line will describe when the activities are to be accomplished. Often a chart can best convey this information.

- **Resources**—The resources section is a justification for any equipment being requested.

- **Evaluation**—There are two kinds of evaluation. The first is the evaluation of results—were the stated objectives met? The second is the evaluation of process—was the original plan adhered to?

- **Dissemination**—This refers to how the program developed with the grant may be shared with others. Helpful dissemination plans include activities, costs, time line, evaluation methods, and any learning experiences that came out of the implementation of the project.

- **Budget**—Budgets involve a lot of research. Everything that could possibly need to be paid for should be included here. List each item. Prioritize the items and adjust for anything that is over the budget of the grant. Be sure to make any changes in the narrative sections of the proposal to accurately reflect the budget, including anything previously left out and cutting anything that needs to be eliminated from the budget.

RESOURCES

THE FOUNDATIONS CENTER

The Foundations Center is an independent national service organization. It was established by foundations to provide an authoritative source of foundation and corporate giving. Collections are located in libraries, community foundations, and other nonprofit agencies throughout the fifty states.

For current information, the toll-free information number is 1-800-424-9836. The Web site is at http://fdncenter.org/.

THE MAIN REFERENCE COLLECTIONS

Foundations Center
8th Floor
79 Fifth Avenue
New York, NY 10003
(212) 620-4230

Foundations Center
Kent H. Smith Library
1422 Euclid, Suite 1356
Cleveland, OH 44115
(216) 861-1933

Foundations Center
312 Sutter Street, Rm. 312
San Francisco, CA 94108
(415) 397-0902

Foundations Center
1001 Connecticut Avenue, NW
Washington, DC 20036
(202) 331-1400

Foundations Center
Suite 150, Grand Lobby
Hurt Building, 50 Hurt Plaza
Atlanta, GA 30303
(404) 880-0094

PUBLICATIONS

Education Grants Alert
(800) 655-5597

Funding Update
Education Funding Resources
11265 Canyon Drive
San Jose, CA 95127-1323
(408) 258-8020

Grant Network Review
Grant Research and Information
256 South Robertson Blvd.
Suite 207
Beverly Hills, CA 90211
(213) 651-7368
e-mail: GrantNet@aol.com

Grants for Schools
Education Retrieval Resource
617 Wright Avenue
Terrytown, LA 70056-4037
(800) 891-6354
Write for a free sample copy.

**GRANTS for School Districs
Monthly Hotline**
(800) 229-2084

DIRECTORIES AND OTHER INFORMATION

Foundation Reporter
Corporate Giving Directory
(800) 877-8238
The Foundation Grants Index
(800) 424-9836

Directory of Major State Foundations
Logos Associates
PO Box 31
Woodsville, NH 03785-0031

Education Funding Research Council
Federal Opportunities Books and Newsletters
(800) 876-0226

Capitol Publishers
Education and Foundation Grants Information
(800) 221-0425

FUNDING SOURCES

The Pew Charitable Trusts
One Commerce Square
2005 Market Street, #1700
Philadelphia, PA 19103

Gifts in Kind America
700 North Fairfax Street, #300
Alexandria, VA 22314

Ford Foundation
320 East 43rd Street
New York, NY 10017

The Prudential Foundation
751 Broad Street, 15th Floor
Newark, NJ 07102

Adobe Systems
Software company
1585 Charleston Rd.
Mountain View, CA 94043
(415) 962-6643

Advanced Logic Research
Personal computer manufacturer
9401 Jeronimo
Irvine, CA 92718
(714) 581-6770

Apple Computer
Hardware and software manufacturer
20525 Mariana Ave., MS 385
Cupertino, CA 95014
(408) 974-2974

AST
Personal computer manufacturer
16215 Alton Parkway
Irvine, CA 92713
(714) 727-4141

Amdahl
Mainframe computers
1250 East Arques Ave., MS 105
Sunnyvale, CA 94088
(408) 746-6000

AT&T Foundations
Telecommunications
PO Box 1430
Wall, NJ 07719
(212) 605-6734

Borland
Software developer
1800 Green Hills Rd.
Scotts Valley, CA 95066
(408) 438-8400

Claris Corporation
Software developer
5201 Patrick Henry Drive
Box 58168
Santa Clara, CA 95052
(408) 987-7000

Compaq Computer Corporation
Personal computers
PO Box 692000
Houston, TX 77269-2000
(713) 374-4625

Digital Equipment Corporation
Voice technology
111 Powdermill Rd., MSO 1-814
Maynard, MA 01754
(508) 493-9210

Epson America, Inc.
Printers, personal computers
20770 Madrona Ave.
Torrance, CA 90503
(213) 782-0770

Hewlett Packard Foundation
Computer printers
3000 Hanover St., PO Box 10301
Palo Alto, CA 94304
(415) 857-1501

IBM
Computer hardware and software
Old Orchard Rd.
Armonk, NY 10504
(914) 765-1900

NEC America
Computer technology
401 Ellis St., P.O. Box 7241, M/V 4102
Mountain View, CA 94039
(415) 960-6000

Tektronix Foundation & Corporate Contributions
Personal computers, printers, terminals
P.O. Box 500
Beaverton, OR 97077
503) 627-7085

Toshiba America Information Systems, Inc.
Laptops, fax machines, photocopiers
1 Bunker Hill
601 W. 5th Street, 4th Floor
Los Angeles, CA 90071
(213) 623-4200

GLOSSARY

A

ASCII: American Standard Code for Information Interchange

assessment: evaluating a product

AUP (acceptable use policy): a document outlining terms and conditions for use of the Internet, signed by parents, students, and teachers

AVI: audio video interleaved—Microsoft's video format for *Windows*

B

bit: binary digit—a transistor or capacitor in a memory cell

BMP: (*Windows* graphic) bitmap; graphics file format

bookmark: option to mark a site location on the Internet

boot: to start a computer (Warm boot restarts a computer without turning it off; cold boot starts a computer from an off state.)

browser: application software which allows user to navigate the World Wide Web (ex., *Netscape*)

bulletin board (BBS): area on the Internet for the user to exchange information with other participants

button: in a multimedia program an object you create to allow action and/or movement to another area of the presentation

byte: 8 bits=1 byte; holds the equivalent of a single character

C

CD-ROM: compact disk-read only memory

clip art: prepared artwork or graphics to cut and paste

clipboard: area in program that holds graphics or text which has been cut or copied

copy: option to duplicate information on clipboard until pasted

CPU: central processing system—brains of the computer

crash: unexpected failure of equipment

cut: option to remove information from document and store on clipboard until pasted

D

default: settings already made in computer programs and on hardware

dialog box: window on the screen from which you make choices

digital camera: camera used to take pictures which are digitized for use on a computer program

DOS: disk operating system

download: to retrieve information, data, files, or pictures from an outside source

E

e-mail(electronic mail): usually brief messages sent and received over computer networks

edit: to make corrections/additions to a document

Ethernet: local area network card in computers connecting them together with cables

GLOSSARY *(cont.)*

F

fax (facsimile): a document transmitted over the telephone via fax machine

font: style of type

format: prepare a disk in platform specific to read or write information

freeware: freely shared, copied, or given software

FTP (file transfer protocol): method of downloading Internet files

G

GIF: graphics interchange format—a graphics format often used for pictures transmitted by modem

GOPHER: Internet software that allows you to look through all kinds of online information

graphics: pictures and images

H

hardware: equipment or peripherals

home page: usually the first page at a World Wide Web site

hot buttons: shortcuts for performing actions (ex., Control S is shortcut for saving.)

HTML (hypertext markup language): World Wide Web programming language

hypertext/hyperlink: in a document or Internet site, highlighted graphic or word which when clicked on will link you to another location

I

icon: pictures on the screen representing files or programs

import: bring information into a document from another location

Internaut: Internet user

Internet service provider (ISP): company/organization providing access to the Internet

J

JPEG: Joint Photographic Experts Group

K

K: kilo = 1,000 (ex., 64 kilobytes or 64,000 bytes)

L

listserv: service a user joins which posts information from members of this service

log on: to sign onto a computer system

M

MOV: a video format

MPEG: an acronym for moving picture expert group: a video format

multimedia: computer presentation that involves images, movies, audio, etc., or a combination of all of the above

GLOSSARY *(cont.)*

N

navigate: move around the Internet

netiquette: conduct rules for Internet use

network: group of connected computers

O

online: means a computer user is connected to the Internet

P

PCX: a bitmapped graphic file format, originally developed for the PC Paintbrush program

peripheral: external device connected to the computer (ex., printer)

PICT: (PICTure) MacIntosh graphics file format (PC version is .PCT)

platform: operating system such as Mac or DOS

public domain: freeware, software available to anyone

Q

QuickTime: software product required to be installed on your computer to run movies

S

search engine: program used to search for information on the Internet (ex., *Yahoo*)

shareware: software which must be purchased after a limited trial period

software: programs/materials used on hardware

surfing: browse about on the Internet

T

telecommunications: communicating with other computers via modem

template: framework that has been prepared and can be completed and Saved As

text: data in the form of words or numbers

text box: space on the card where text can be typed

TIFF: tagged image file format, a graphics file format

transitions: ways to move from one card to another

trash/recycle bin: ways to get rid of unwanted information

U

undo: reverses the last action taken

upgrade: install newer, usually more powerful, software

V

virus: software program which intentionally sabotages another program, computer, or network

virtual reality: computer simulated environment which appears to be real

W

WAV: windows sound file (one minute of sound = 644K to 5 mg)

World Wide Web: a system of html pages which are interconnected via hyperlinks

TECHNOLOGY BOOKS AND RESOURCES

Barron, Ann E. and Gary W. Orwig. *New Technologies for Education—A Beginner's Guide.* Libraries Unlimited, 1995.

Healey, Deborah. *Something to Do on Tuesday.* Athelstan, 1995.

Holmes, Kathleen and Don Rawitsch. *Evaluating Technology-Based Instructional Programs—An Educator's Guide.* Texas Center for Educational Technology, 1993.

Rathje, Linda, Jill Heyerly & Becky Schenck. *ClarisWorks for Students.* HRS Publication, 1995.

Reidl, Joan. *The Integrated Technology Classroom—Building Self-Reliant Learners.* Allyn & Bacon, 1995.

Sharp, Vicki F. *HyperStudio in One Hour.* ISTE, 1994.

Wetzel, Keith and Suzanne Painter. *Microsoft Works 3.0 for the Macintosh—A Workbook for Educators.* ISTE, 1994.

Willing, Kathlene R. and Suzanne Girard. *Learning Together—Computer Integrated Classrooms.* Pembroke Publishers Ltd., 1990.

Wodaski, Ron. *Absolute Beginner's Guide to Multimedia.* Sams Publishing, 1994.

Yoder, Sharon and David Moursund. *Introduction to ClarisWorks—A Tool for Personal Productivity.* ISTE, 1993.

Yoder, Sharon and Irene Smith. *Looking Good! The Elements of Document Design for Beginners.* ISTE, 1995.

Magazines

The Computing Teacher
ISTE
1787 Agate Street
Eugene, Oregon 97043

MultiMedia Schools
462 Danbury Road
Wilton, CT 06897-9819

Technology and Learning
PO Box 49727
Dayton, Ohio 45449